Entrepreneurship

Philosophia

Love of Business Wisdom

Joshua Okello

Entrepreneurship
Philosophia
The Love of Business Wisdom

Joshua Okello
2016

First printing: 2016

ISBN-13: 978-1523664726

ISBN-10:152366472X

Joshua Okello
www.joshokello.com

For Jared

CONTENTS

Introduction

One thing that a leader should know, understand, and equip him/herself with is a good grasp of philosophy. Philosophy is the study of ultimate nature of understanding reality and existence in the actual world today. It is said that the term philosophy (*philosophia* in Greek) was first coined by Pythagoras, a thinker, a scientist and a philosopher. *Entrepreneurship Philosophia* is a book that explicitly talks about the intellectual understanding of the virtue of knowledge in entrepreneurial realms.

As appealing as that definition is, this book talks about entrepreneurship and leadership philosophy, what is required of a leader and an entrepreneur to do to see full expected results. It is impossible to talk about philosophy without touching on Greek Philosophers. Most of them are considered to be the fathers of modern philosophy, therefore, it would be unfair to write this book without mentioning some influential characters in modern as well as early philosophy.

Plato, Socrates, Xenophon, Pythagoras are among the early contributors of modern philosophy. Most of their works have a unique pattern of reasoning, proslogion, meditations and argumentative techniques that baffled their audiences. A leader must be a lover of wisdom, must be devoted towards achieving excellence through truth and must pursue virtuousness alongside his subject goals. Philosophy is the constant pursuit of the virtue of wisdom.

Wisdom, excellence, truth and decorum require intrinsic understandings from omniscience. This does not mean that leaders must be all knowing, but should be logical in their reasoning. Leaders should be people who can support their arguments with valid premises. Good philosophy is good wisdom that results in good leadership.

Leaders, according to this book, should be educated people. By education, I do not mean the general knowledge-injection-process in modern and formal learning but rather the ability to transform the invisible into visible materials, the ability to draw a vision and create a plan that helps people to work towards achieving their objectives. This is the intrinsic knowledge that a leader is expected to have.

This book also simplifies the philosophy of success that is required of every leader in the market today and in the future. It offers explanations with examples and breaks down the complex concepts into easy and understandable contexts that, if well implemented, can lead to success. So is success that important? Or is there anything that we should always strive towards?

This book reflects on time as the most valuable gift we have. Therefore it encourages leaders to always appreciate and increase the value of their time. Of all the advice you can benefit from, pay attention to what this book says about failure. A lot of potential leaders and entrepreneurs fail to try because of their fear of failure but by the end of reading this book, you will learn what failure means in the entrepreneurial world.

As I invite you to embrace this journey with me, I would like to first highlight some important reasons and wishes that I have especially in the field of entrepreneurial leadership.

i. It is important not to take issues personally, but rather to engage in personal issues that further the growth of humanity. Addressing these issues is important but only when done in love. Therefore, let everyone play their role to the best of his or her understanding and never be the barrier that hinders a devoted group from success and happiness.

ii. It is critical to understand that as long as we can think rationally, we can achieve anything we set our minds on. It requires hard and smart work. It is important to use reason or our faculty of logic, but it is something totally different to implement our ideas.

iii. I did not write this book to express bravado, pride, intellect or book earned wisdom, carelessness or arrogance as most pundits do in our societies today. My goal is to stay humble, do my part for the common good of the people.

iv. Apart from leadership and entrepreneurship, I will continue to take part in the philosophical life serving our divine creator in actualization of His divine works that present opportunities to serve one another in Christ's name.

v. I remain a servant of the people, putting aside all the hard earned success that was given either by efforts of fellow mortals or by immortal.

vi.   All leaders, entrepreneurs and philosophers will stay true to themselves not changing with time, emotions due to external pains, sorrows, happiness, success or anything that impact our life leading to realizable change in the way we deal with fellow mortals, but rather to keep our faculty and maxim of good philosophy same at all times unless changing for the best.

vii.   Good philosophy will be a creed to both aspiring and incumbent leaders, entrepreneurs, philosophers and anybody else whose faculty directs towards good knowledge also called "the truth."

        In the past, I have mentioned repeatedly that success is infinite and so is failure. A lot of people choose and by choose I mean deeply embrace the intentional acts of failure. Yes, we fail intentionally, and the few who are successful also succeed intentionally. Success is the single prey that every hunter is going for. It is important then to be strong; fast enough to catch it before any hunter pawns on it, but it is also important to be generous enough to share success with fellow hunters. Those who succeed, do so because they are always ready to help others catch the prey and in return other people help them back. That is the common philosophy of success.

        This sounds easy, but it is not as easy as it sounds. Success is pain while failure is pleasure. Success is denial while failure is to have and it is to have in abundance. The only major difference between the two is that success has a lot of hurdles while failure is packed with easy things that sweep you away into defeat.

        Then there is the Mega Success. This is what I call the infinite victory, it is the repeated achievement, and the limitless prosperity in anything you put your mind and heart into. Mega Success is easy to attain but only if you can stand the torrents that the first and second attempts at success bring to you. While the majority lies in mediocre success, a lot of people choose not to attempt the initial stages of success. These are some of the things that lead to stagnation of success.

        Those who are smart are smart enough to know that mediocre success simply means mediocre failure. Any moment you settle for mediocrity, you will remain mediocre forever. Go into the game with a mentality that you are a winner, strive to excel. Do all you can to succeed but above all, focus ahead. How is whatever you are doing at the present leading you to mega success? If staying on social media purposelessly takes your time, this is the time to cut it off. These are some of the practices that lead to Mega Success.

Trust

Deceptions are short lived. Don't do it! Be a man of integrity, your reputation is more important than anything else. There is no shortcut to success, therefore, do not cheat. Be honest even if it means you are going to lose. A victory won dishonestly is as bad as a defeat. It is not worth celebrating, and it does not bring the contentment of achieving a big dream. Be trustworthy and nothing else.

And as Francis Bacon once said; Read not to contradict and confute, nor to believe and take for granted, nor to find talk and discourse, but to weigh and consider. Some books are to be tasted, others to be swallowed, and some few to be chewed and digested: that is, some books are to be read only in parts, others to be read, but not curiously, and some few to be read wholly, and with diligence and attention.

On Keeping Minutes and Losing Hours

Time is a sort of river of passing events, and strong is its currents; no sooner is a thing brought to sight than it is swept by and another takes its place and this too will be swept away ~ Marcus Aurelius.

Time destroys the falls opinions, but he confirms judgements of nature ~ Cicero.

Time is the most unknown in all unknown things ~ Aristotle.

Meetings are events where minutes are kept and hours lost. Let your team work.

In our office, we always have a weekly meeting mostly on Tuesday mornings. We give updates on the projects, plan for the future, brainstorm on new ideas, invite guest speakers to motivate our team and address any internal issues that need to be resolved.

Our team comes to the office to work, not for meetings. There is only one meeting every week. The rest of the week I just walk in different departments any day at any time to ask if they are grappling with any challenges as they work on the projects. It takes me at most ten minutes to walk round in all our organization's departments. One thing I try never to let happen is for an employee to ask me to clarify what they are working on; if this happens then I know I am not doing my work properly.

We are a team of four people in our office; if we all meet for three hours, that is twelve hours of productivity lost. Practically, that is already one day of work lost. Our value statement is to create value at all times. If we lose twelve hours a day of work in 5 days, that is sixty hours of work going to waste in exchange for minutes.

This is the reason why we decided only to have meetings once a week. When you are organising meetings, and this is one thing I learned the hard way working with my board members, make sure that you have your agenda ready, and the agenda must be of value to both the organizations and employees involved. Never call a meeting without a good reason for having one.

On Mega Success and Boot Strapping

Who works, has no time to a prank. And the truth is that work kills off the vices that are born by idleness ~ Seneca.

Who doesn't apply himself to business, won't achieve much success ~ Xunzi

If we begin with certainties, we shall end in doubts; but if we begin with doubts, and are patient in them, we shall end in certainties ~ Francis Bacon

Do you have an idea of value? An idea that you can sell? An idea that can be bought? Is it an idea that can transform lives? How does your idea impact emotions? Research has shown that people buy from emotions and emotions can only be conveyed through a story. So what is your story? Boot Strapping is by itself an amazing story to convince anybody to buy into your idea. Bootstrapping is starting a business or an organization without much money. A lot of entrepreneurs start this way. What makes one successful and what makes another one a mega success?

If almost all entrepreneurs start from zero, how do they get to one? It is not easy. It is demanding. It is tiring and it does not need people who are faint of heart. This is why almost all businesses fail before seeing the second yearbook close. However, there is no need of putting all your energy into something for a few days and then quitting. You have all it takes to achieve mega success. So let's start with the reason why people fail in life.

Nobody was born a failure but failure is a mindset. It is a self-inflicted pain that we happily choose to live with, but there are better ways to improve our lives. Here are some of the ways that lead to failure:

Lack of Ideas

To lack an idea to put your efforts in is to lack a big understanding of humanity. When you want to generate ideas, look around you. What is wrong? What needs improvement? What can the world do differently? And how can you be the only source of achieving this? Take for example; the world has used enough trees to make furniture, how about designing furniture using recycled plastic? That is a great idea that will revolutionize the world and it is something that has been done. Now ask yourself, how can you do it better, cheaper and efficiently? How about using gravitational force to generate energy? There is enough gravitational force to produce metric watts of energy but how do we harvest the gravitational potential energy?

If your circumstances are not pushing you towards starting something new, then you must be too comfortable with the conditions that life throws at you. Mega success is achieved when you turn your misfortunes into fortunes. Creativity will lead you to develop new ideas and new ideas will lead to a change in the realm that advances humanity.

Self-Doubt

Not all doubts are bad; some doubts can actually help you improve your performance to attain mega success. Let us divide doubt into two sections: a). Good doubts b). Bad doubts.

a) *Good doubts* – These are the gut-wrenching thoughts and systematic skepticisms about the truths of one's efforts to achieve a mega success. If your doubt pushes you towards trying things that are greater than you, then you have good doubts. With good doubts, you are challenging and competing with yourself and not with anybody else. They are there to set you apart from any other person by improving your standards of performance.

b) *Bad Doubts* – These are doubts that lead to automatic failure. Mostly they originate from asking "what ifs." The best they can offer you is to discourage you from trying. A bad doubt magnifies a problem and in self-defense, it convinces you to stay aloof from the issue. It has strong convincing powers that you are better and safer not trying than to try and fail.

Therefore in this section we are going to focus on the latter doubt; the bad doubt. To defeat self-doubt, you have to reason beyond the doubt. Logic can be a no-brainer to some people while to others it is a hard task. It comes when you have a strong self-belief therefore, you must first learn that everything is possible. We can all achieve our dreams if we put our thoughts and efforts on them.

Bad Influence

You cannot go to Mars if Elon Musk does not influence you. You cannot run an airplane business if you are not a fan of Richard Branson. You cannot be successful in the stock market if you are not a strong follower of Warren Buffet. You cannot be successful in computer and software business if you are not a fan of Steve Jobs and Bill Gates. What is it that they did that made them unique? Find out what drives them and closely write your philosophy in relation to what they have done. That is the first step towards Mega success. If you have a positive influence, you will also influence positively and if you have a negative influence, you will also influence negatively.

Mega success relies on your first 5 best friends. If they are not Mega achievers, then you are most likely going to be like them. Those who have attained mega success like to work and support those with the mega success type of mindset but first, you have to prove to them that you can handle mega success. That is the most difficult hurdle, but it can be done.

Lack of Determination

Bootstrapping is never easy. It is an energy drainer. It takes time, and it is easy to find yourself a stranger in your own world, a hopeless, lonely loser who has no friends and family. Bootstrapping requires higher determination. Running a business is easy but starting and growing a business from zero to one is a hurdle. It is a task that leaves most people mentally and physically drained. Try to do something new and you will realize how petty your ideas are. You will be rejected more than 99 times, but if you try again, maybe you might get lucky with a hundredth attempt. That is enough failure to discourage no matter what.

If you can handle all criticisms, rejections, discouragements and lack of stable income that every bootstrapper gets in the first year, then know that you have the potential of achieving mega success. Mega success has got mega hurdles that if you can safely go through, then you can emerge victoriously. Never give up.

Dream-preneurs

These are the people with big dreams that never come true. They can visualize mega success and act it, but they are too reluctant to start it. Dream-preneurs can be great leaders if they find a team to build the chemistry with. What I do not understand is why they fail to act. They can break down a strategy of how they are going to start a mega project and even give you timeline. Meet them seven years later; the dream will have grown with zero actions taken. Dream-preneurs fear risk-taking, and that is what keeps them stagnant forever. Simple advice to this group of people; never live a Wall Street or Silicon Valley life if you are not there yet.

On Building a Cohesive Organization

Building a cohesive leadership team is the first critical step that an organization must take if it is to have the best chance at success ~Patrick Lencioni

Nothing is as tiring as being a personal assistant to an entrepreneur. Even though I have not been a personal assistant to any businessperson before, I have had personal assistants and the truth is, I never feel like we are at the same frequency. Even though God blessed me with an intelligent team to work with, it is never enough for an entrepreneur.

Entrepreneurs are idea generators; they are think tanks and vision casters who see the big picture. Besides, they are dreamers. They can visualize the invisible. They can breathe life in mortal objects. They see possibility in every situation, good or bad.

This could be a great blessing to them but on the other side it can be a curse if not well communicated. To build a cohesive organization, there must be fluid communication flowing from top down and bottom up. As an entrepreneur and a leader, it is beneficial to know every section of an organization and their functions.

The Visionary

In my book *Strategies of Entrepreneurial Leadership*, the visionary is compared to the Hawks. They can see for miles, they are agile, wise and accurate. The visionary can be stubborn; they are broadcasters of dreams and influencers of people. The visionary paves the way and lays foundations for all to follow. Nothing makes them as happy as seeing their ideas coming to fruition.

However, most visionary people get frustrated a lot because they generate great ideas but do not put them down in writing. This complicates their ideas, making it very hard for people to follow. Since they see the big picture, they assume that turning their ideas into reality is as easy as generating the ideas but this is not true. It takes skill, effort, commitment, energy, and dedication to ensure that the implementations of ideas are done well.

This explains why the most visionary and sharp of all the fish in the tanks end up leading frustrated lives. Lack of systematic plan of implementation is always their weakness and that is why they need managers who are good at planning. This is not to say that all entrepreneurs are like this but a greater percentage of them fall into this category. There are also great entrepreneurs who have built successful organizations single-handedly before they are joined by teams.

The visionaries are the heads; they are the sailors, the captains of their ships and the pilots of their jets. The success and failure of their organization rely solely on them and this is why it is important that they are great leaders and good stewards of time.

The Implementers

The implementers are the right-hand men and women of the visionary people. In heaven, they would be the cherubim or the worker bees on earthly terms. Once a destination is set, they pave the way for the followers to follow. They are the rolling wheels since they move the organization therefore it is important that they be people of dignity. They should be wisely chosen and, if possible, handpicked to implement mega success.

Once the vision is shared with them, they can plan and act swiftly to see the dreams come true. The visionary team should hold the implementers dear to their hearts to get them trapped to their vision. As a start-up, it is common not to find the right people on the first attempt, be quick to fire and slow to hire for these are the people who determine your success as an entrepreneur. Treat implementers with care, keep them but above all, make sure that they do their work. You do not want to keep parasites that gobble at the little profits you make.

The Followers

These are your fanatics, they are your diehards. They can defend you in every situation. They are ready to go in the ditch with you. They will climb the tall mountains with you, cross the deep oceans with you and at times even dare to jump in the fire with you. As long as they can sense good leadership, a man of big dreams and a game changer then they can stay with you forever.

It takes a while to gather such a following. These are people who do not only believe in you, but see you as the cult-head. They believe in you, your efforts, strengths and vision. To gather such a cult-like following, a leader must share with them the vision and show them how this vision will change their lives.

It is hectic to follow a visionless person. It becomes hopeless and people turn their backs to search for an alternative very fast. Followers can get desperate to a point where anything that comes their way, no matter how bad it is, as long as they get rid of you as a leader then they will flock to that.

It is never hard to turn things around in such cases. Listening to your followers and recognizing their complaints can take you far.

Cohesion

To build cohesion, these three groups must all be in line. They should share a common goal, the vision and mission should be their binding factor. A selling point to all the leaders I know and still will be for another millennium to come is the "change." People will always want a change, either a change from the norm, economic, social, and spiritual or behaviour.

Change is such a powerful word that triggers enthusiasm in everybody. People will always strive to make their community better and it takes a leader with a mindset to bring that change. Followers adore people who believe and are confident in the change they are preaching about. They not only read a lot in a leader's words but how his body language portrays his beliefs in his utterances. Preach the change to garner support but above all, remember to build cohesion to make these changes come true.

On Discipline as Enthusiasm with Direction

A disciplined mind leads to happiness and an undisciplined mind leads to suffering ~ Dalai Lama

We are what we repeatedly do, excellence then is not an act, but a habit ~ Aristotle
Rule your mind, or it will rule you ~ Horace

Entrepreneurship needs discipline otherwise it is enthusiasm without direction.

We can create all the amazing visions, plans, strategies and dreams but those are the most worthless wealth we own if we do not transform them to practicality. We can develop business plans but fail to implement them. This has happened so many times to me.

Some of my early entrepreneurship included vegetable farming, poultry and music production. All these started well, generated some revenue but died after a short while. I had no business stamina, but I was fond of starting new businesses. This is something common with most entrepreneurs. They are good idea generators, but some of them do not do well in implementing their findings.

I worked on learning music production for two years, built a studio in my bedroom and during this time, I was in university. It was probably the most enjoyable and memorable part of my life as a business student. After mastering the music production, I wrote a business plan, named my business J-Heights Productions, produced for friends at the University and wrote my own songs. I further produced an album and launched it. I sold some and gave out almost 200 copies then I lost interest in music production consequently selling my music label.

This is not a decision that I regret in any way but it taught me a lot. First on perseverance. I learned that nothing comes easy and it takes work to maintain a business. Many people would consider this a failure but to me, this was a stepping-stone towards success. It was a learning opportunity where I learned a lot about real life business, more than I learned in my two years in university.

One thing that happens when you start a business is that people start to associate you with your brand and what you do. Today, I still meet people who ask me if I have released a new album and it is disappointing to tell them that I quit music. However I also offer them another deal and that is my literature.

Since they already know about my creativity, they can relate to it and enjoy my style of writing; they have the same hope that my books will be entertaining, educational and meditative as use to be the case with my music.

Creating a business is not hard anybody can create one. But it requires guts to take your product out there, get rejected and still continue to do what you do because you know the value it creates. By continuing to do what you do best, you will start creating loyal followers. This is all that matters in every business. To gain loyal followers, you must be loyal to your business too.

Work hard and follow your plan. Nothing is as important as a building and structuring your own work rhythm. In 2014, I set a goal to meet 365 inspiring leaders in 365 days. Most of the things that we discussed with these leaders were success, failures, how to start and come up with a vision, what to do when things do not go your way and what it takes to be a great leader.

80% of the leaders I met did not agree that they were leaders but they all believed in hard work. 25% of these leaders believed in creating life rhythm. 95% talked about failure as something to be expected on your journey to success. What struck me most was the percentage that talked about creating life rhythm.

A rhythm is a pattern of life that you lead. It involves; the work you do, how you do it, time with family, time with friends, time for fun, etc. How do you allocate your time? What is your daily schedule like? Do you have a rhythm? If not create one. Never plan to live but rather live to plan.

On Success Behind Failure

Success is stumbling from failure to failure with no loss of enthusiasm ~ Winston Churchill

It is stupid to become unhappy, because of possibilities to become unhappy someday ~ Seneca

No matter how many times you fall, get back up and continue the fight. Failure is the only thing guaranteed in this world, but for success you have to overcome all the failures. This means that as a leader and a philosopher, you do not have to quit for mega success hides behind failures.

The common example that has been widely used by almost every writer in the world today is Thomas Edison and the light bulb experiment. His famous quote "I only learned that there are 10,000 ways to do something wrong" comes after his numerous attempts to build a light bulb. He later on found out that there is only one way to do it. In leadership, finding this one way can be an odious task.

People are always scared of failing and losing everything they have but really, when we came to this earth, we brought nothing with us and when dust turns back to dust, we will go with nothing. It does not matter if we have expensive gold or silver on our caskets. At that very moment when the breath of life is taken away from us, we go with nothing and just remain empty shells that are worth nothing.

At that stage, it will not matter how much you knew, how important you were, how poor you were or how intelligent you were. It will not even matter how much your bank statement read at that moment. All the luxurious homes and vehicles you own become worthless. So what is the benefit of accumulating all these wealth?

A lot of people deny themselves the adventure of living like business people. Having been a socio-capitalist entrepreneur, nothing is as fun as dealing with stress and overcoming it successfully. Nothing is as great as going to bed an achiever. It is true you will fail, but failure by itself is not a valid reason to deny yourself great opportunities that you do not take steps towards.

Being an avid soccer fan, I enjoy watching FIFA World Cup games. At the end of the game there is only one country, one team that takes the trophy home. For them, to get the gold medal, it takes one person who is a great risk taker to take the shot at the goal. In soccer, there is the opposite defence team, a goalkeeper and enough barriers to stop you from scoring. There is also the pressure of taking shots that go the wrong way. Remember the whole world is watching what they are doing with the ball. But all these never stop them from taking the attempts.

Get ready to fail for that is how one can know the dos and don'ts in business. A leader is not a leader unless he or she is a risk taker. Leaders are great cowards who can put on a brave face and confront their fears. The fear of failure is not an excuse not to go an extra mile. Great people in the history of success failed so many times and that is how they got promoted to be in the top echelons in societies.

Mega Success Means Mega War

Coming together is a beginning, keeping together is progress,
working together is success ~ Henry Ford

A man may do an immense deal of good, if he does not care
who gets the credit for it ~ Father Strickland

Life is a battle and mega success is a mega war, try and win both. Mega success is there to defeat you unless you battle it stronger than the challenges it poses. To win big, you must have a strategy and an army to help you fight.

One of my business mentors once told me that to be a millionaire, you only need a million friends and ask them for a dollar each and there you go. It is that easy but I guarantee you that winning a million friends is not easy, let alone asking them for a dollar. Since this is the easiest way that has been proved to be close to impossible, you are only left with a number of ways to attain mega success.

To get to mega success you need an army. It does not matter how big or small they are but how well they fight. It is important to know that your army's total output return is directly proportional to your total engagement in the battle. The more you are involved, the more your army will do. So who are these armies?

Mentors

Try and have at least one mentor and if possible have more. It is the philosophy of mega success. If you are going to an action, act big and think of success as infinite.

Once you establish a rapport with mentors, they will be your guides, they will prophesy the future for you and they will show you what not to do. This point is very important. Mentors will not only be there to advise you on the best but they will also discourage you from doing what is not right. You will very quickly learn from them that they do not like the easy way. Shortcuts are short-lived. Take note on what your mentors tell you is wrong and evaluate it. Maybe some ideas might only need a little tweaking. Make sure that you explicitly tell them your plan, that all of them understand your goal and how to get there. This is one branch of an army that is very important.

Employees

These are your direct teams. You engage with them every single day. They will make you or break you. In this case, be slow to hire and quick to fire. That might sound harsh but as a startup or as a stable business, you do not need liabilities. You should expect your employees to do their part in building your organization. Try and use the law of diminishing returns to boost your team's productivity.

Your team should be there for the fun of working with you and your goals and not for money. You want people who can stand with you for two months without pay and here is the sad news; they are very rare on this planet. Find people who love their job not those who work because they have to. Still, you must be prepared to spend more hours in your office working late and starting early.

Board Members

It can be so much fun to work with board members and it can also be very painful to work with board members. Board members do less but are more powerful than you are even when you are the founder and CEO of the company. This happens for a reason, their main role is to keep you accountable. Ninety-eight percent of the work will be on your shoulders, your board only gets two percent and most of the time it is when they have to inspect your financial books.

However, you can increase these two percent to over fifteen percent if you know how to work your crowd. It requires charm and good people skills. Know that your board members know other successful people that can help you with new ideas. They cannot know how much help you need if you do not ask. Ask them as many questions as possible and try to involve them in a number of ways that are not too demanding to help you grow to mega success. They will be happy to help you and that is why they agreed to be on your board anyway.

But remember never to offend them because they will fire you. That is not a joke!

Fan Base

Build a fan base, people who are crazy in love with you, those who are willing to follow you even if you are driving them straight into a lake of fire. Lure those who are willing to travel across the country just to hear you speak. The easiest way to do this is by caring for humanity. People love those who care, especially those who genuinely care.

Be loved for your works. Inspire people to do more and let people learn their intrinsic value. Correct where necessary but always give thanks. Nothing beats a genuine thank you. You are working with fellow human beings therefore be a human too. Share your ideas and educate people and people will freely educate you.

If you can coordinate all these people to be in harmony, resonating well with your goals then you are destined to attain mega success. Mega success does not just come; it requires mega work. It is a mega battle that must be fought and won.

On Missing Great Opportunities

We are all faced with a series of great opportunities brilliantly disguised as impossible situations ~ Charles Swindoll.

Iron rusts from disuse, water loses its purity from stagnation even so does inaction sap the vigour of the mind ~ Leonardo Da Vinci.

You are risk-free outside of entrepreneurship, but you miss great opportunities. A lot of people tend to shy away from business either because it is hectic, complex, involves a lot of math, has got so many failures, or even fear of success. The latter point will be discussed later in this book.

Germany is widely known for her classy technology. Most cars from Germany are expensive, a symbol of class, and swagger of life. That is what they take their pride in. Germany is also known to be a country that manufactures and ships other aquatic vessels. They have succeeded in doing that. To test their technology against any other competitor, they have to set their ships in deep sea waters to navigate around the globe. We all know the dangers involved with large bodies of water, from tsunamis, tidal waves, icebergs to dangerous aquatic animals. All these challenges do not stop them from sending their vessels out in the water.

They know that their ships are safe at the dock but they choose to send them in the deep seas and oceans because that is what they were made for.

It is also the same with entrepreneurship and/or leadership. Leaders were not created to stay in offices. Even though it is safe to stay in the office or not start your own business, you are missing out on great opportunities.

Some people will go as far as listing for you vessels that sank and caused dangers to those who boarded them. Think of the great Titanic, think of the Noronic disaster, a ship that burst into flames and claimed lives in Lake Ontario. Do you remember the Malaysian airplane that disappeared in space to date? We have a choice of not taking any action towards success for the fear of challenges that might arise. It is also easy to sit back and relax and watch things happen with a hope that you are safe and that nothing can come your way, but you can be assured of one thing and that is; you deny yourself great opportunities.

Any moment you fail to take an action that could have changed your life or any other person's life, you will live to regret those moments. In any leadership position, one ought to know that you cannot lose what you do not have. Whatever your dream is, if you do not get it, be proud of yourself for you did your best. Only the conditions did not favour you, and you have nothing much to lose.

Opportunities only come once anything else is a second chance. From this phrase we can say that our first chance was when we were born. We should consider anything we are doing today as another opportunity that this beautiful life has granted us. Work like it is your last day on earth and if it is going to school, study like this is the only chance you've got. If you are a leader, lead like you are not going to lead again.

Take everything you are doing as though you are doing it for Jesus. If Jesus was to inspect everything you did for him in the evening, what would he say? Would he be satisfied with your work? Or would he be disgusted by what you did? The answer fully lies in your hands. Choose to be perfect and aim for it. You might not be wholly perfect as it is nearly impossible to achieve excellent scores in whatever you are doing but show responsibility and be proactive. Work to impress, do not work to depress.

Every great idea we see out there is because somebody took a major step to transform the ideas into action. If Albert Einstein did not try more than ten thousand times to make a light bulb, we could not be having light to date but due to his bold steps, we can be proud and boast of his success today.

Imagine the dangers involved in using electricity to produce light for the first time. He knew very well that he was putting his life on the brink but that did not stop him. He knew that he was safer not taking any action towards building a light bulb but he chose to go against all the odds.

Our minds always rush into negativity, failures, and embarrassments, but one thing we forget is that failures only last for a moment, success lives forever. When I was a student, I failed so many times; I failed in relationships and at the workplace. I disappointed my family but I never lost hope. I knew that my failures, disappointments, and pain were only going to last for a moment. Maybe you might be going through some of the things I have listed above but they only last for hours, days, weeks, months and at most a year. If you never pay attention to the failure and focus on success then you are moving in the right direction.

To say that failing is good does not mean that you just have to sit and watch time pass by. That is irresponsible failing and it is very different from failing after hard work.

One thing I told myself that I would never do in my life is living with regrets. I make decisions once and take situations the way they come. If I fail then I know that failures are part of success and someday

I will have to succeed. Regrets waste my time, time that could be invested in doing something practical. It does not add any value to my life nor does it add any value to people I am serving. Success is a mentality and so is failure. If you consider yourself a failure before you even try, that is who you will be. Before I go to rest with my saviour, I want to look back in life and say that I came without anything and before I leave I want to ensure that; I left something that is of great value to a generation coming after me. That is my goal and that is what success means to me.

Success is adding value in other people's lives. Ask yourself if your actions impact other people's lives positively. Be engaging; build compassion, show love and act on that love. After all, why generate great ideas that could revolutionize the world and not act on them? We are the shapers of our fortune; we need to have faith both in God and in what we believe in for it to come true. You cannot and will never achieve anything you do not believe in.

As much as you are safer doing nothing, it is better to take risks, do something you have never done before. Ask yourself, "when is the last time you did something for the first time?" Do the impossible, for doing the possible gets boring after some time. Above all, remember that you are either generating or degenerating. Choose wisely.

On Reality

What shall we say about those spectators, then, who can see a plurality of beautiful things, but not beauty itself, and who are incapable of following if someone else tries to lead them to it, and who can see many moral actions, but not morality itself, and so on? That they only ever entertain beliefs, and do not know any of the things they believe? ~ Plato

Time destroys the false opinions but he confirms judgements of nature ~ Cicero

There is a big difference between wanting mega success and attaining mega success. The latter appeals to so many but very few keep it real. We have all heard of people changing their dreams to reality, dreams come true and other fancy words they used to describe their achievements. It is good to achieve success but best when you attain mega success.

What is Mega Success Reality?

All ideas, businesses, leaderships and entrepreneurial opportunities originate from the brain. They never start in bedrooms and basements as people say. Once an idea strikes you, the ability to transform that idea into an existing achievement is the reality.

A lot of ideas that we generate totally go to waste, actually up to 80% of constructive and life-transforming ideas are wasted annually. In the movie Matrix, Neo sees a lady in red dress. This is part of the dream, even though the lady in the red dress does not exist in the real world, he can tell how beautiful she is because her image is vivid in his mind.

That is how most life transforming visions come. They are not real when they are in your mind therefore you can talk about them, ignore them or act towards making them a reality. Otherwise, they will be the beautiful girl in red dress in a movie rolling in your brain.

How real is real?

It is surprising that I dreamt about this chapter, woke up and tried to remember and write it down but it was all gone. I went back to bed again and had the very same dream. I was lecturing a philosophy class in a university on Forms by Plato when I decided to change my topic to reality. So how do we transform Forms into substance? Or are we also engulfed in a jail of language and linguistic nonsense where we can pretend to describe substances and fail to understand the true meaning of what we are describing. Are we born with a priori knowledge of everything we know and if so why don't we all become successful in the fields we chose?

When I say, "Coca-Cola can", you create the image of a Coca-Cola can, you build the colors and fonts in your mind, and you can also recall the taste of Coca-Cola in your mouth. That is how powerful our imaginations are and visions are exactly like that. Even though you are not holding a coke can in your hand, you can see it in your mind. Now if you do not go to a shop or to a vending machine and purchase one, then the image of Coca-Cola will be there and might even trigger your taste buds to go and get some. When you transform that strong need for Coca-Cola into actually holding a can and drinking it, you have transformed your dreams into reality.

Mega success is a form that should by all means be transformed into substance. Mega success is like the beautiful girl in the red dress in the movie Matrix. She is charming and you cannot live without giving her a second look. The only thing is that she is not real until you actually wake up. Our minds have that power to transform ideas into illusions and then when we are conscious, we can act on changing them to exist.

We need to learn the forms ahead of time and learning about forms can only take us far. We also need to learn how to change the forms to reality, things that do exist. That is when we move from being successful to mega success.

On building Social Media Kingdom

Before you become a leader, success is all about growing yourself, When you become a leader, success is all about growing others ~ Jack Welch

He who has never learned to obey can never be a good commander ~ Aristotle

The power of the internet is one of the greatest blessings that potential leaders as well as true leaders can count on. It has made sharing of wisdom easy and expansion of one's geographical influence much more possible than it used to be during pre-internet era. To build a true social media platform a leader needs to:

Garner following

My main social media platform is twitter and I am having over 100,000 people following me. These people have contributed to my social media success having been listed as top 50 most influential twitter users in North America.

Create Value

If we truly value ourselves, we will share value with others. All my tweets are tweets that build people. Over 100,000 people who follow me expect positive tweets from me and that is what I do. Not that they control what I have to say on social media but I tweet my thoughts as they come to me. Once your followers know what you tweet about, they will develop a habit of checking your website and interact with your information either internally or externally. I always direct people to my twitter handle when they need motivation or when they are down and depressed. This would be compared to creating a market niche. Who are the people you want to impact with your message? You do not even have to write the wisest tweet all the time. Just tweet about your life but remember never to spam your followers. Too much of anything is dangerous.

Interact

Never just post your ideas, let people know that you are not a robot. We cannot generate positive ideas at all times. Human beings have highs and lows and let your followers see both sides of you. This is called humanizing your social media platform.

Another way to humanize your social media platform is by asking questions. A good example is when I was looking for an editor, I posted on my twitter and within five minutes, my twitter was buzzing with suggestions on some of the most prolific editors in the world of book publishing.

I also use twitter to outsource my mundane tasks. This way, I am creating employment opportunities making people trust that I am not a robot but a real human being.

Spend Time

To build a true social media platform, you have to spend time on it. Spending time does not mean wasting time. I spend 30-45 minutes everyday building and improving, my website, Twitter, Facebook and blog. I also like to follow people who follow me and I do it in person because they mean a lot to me and because they are not worth a robotic response.

Solve a Problem

My blog posts and Twitter ideas are mostly on how to be a better leader and how we can constantly improve to greatness. Every weekend I have a Q&A session where people ask me questions pertaining to leadership and entrepreneurship. If they are open ended questions that need more than 140 characters, then I try to give my followers solutions on my blog joshokello.com. A good part of solving problems is that I also get to ask questions and often times, my followers are open and honest with me which I really appreciate. People will follow you if you show that you care. Care just a little bit more.

Be consistent

When you want to build a true platform, you have to be consistent. If it is posting once or twice a week, be disciplined to do exactly that. Create a social media rhythm and let people know when you are available for them. In my case, I only respond to questions on weekends and my followers know that.

It is also important to be consistent with your content. You do not want to tweet or blog about soccer today, rugby tomorrow and health the following day. It doesn't quite connect. Pick one topic and be disciplined at educating your followers on the same.

Let people know you for one thing and be perfect at it. Above all, give solutions and if you do not have any, then refer your audience to where they can source the information they need because we are not all-knowing.

Be Ready to Learn

The best way to humanize your social media is to ask questions. We are not all knowing and you must accept the fact that some people out there know more than you do. Give them a chance to educate you and educate the world after gaining wisdom from them. The world likes those who listen therefore pay attention to others and consume only those thoughts that build you and your social media community.

On Running with Leadership

The heaviest penalty for declining to rule is to be ruled by someone inferior to yourself ~ Plato

The Philosopher whose dealings are with divine order himself acquires the characteristics of order and divinity ~ Plato

There are only two things in business, you either run with it or run from it. One of the things I learned as I wrote this book is the importance of "choice" in our lives. I realize that in everything we do, there is a decision to be made. How do you make your decision?

Think of one of the greatest leaders you admire either radical or conservative. Those are the people who made tough choices to be who they are. Some were influenced by other great leaders, some were influenced by the environment they lived in, and some were influenced by their cultures and life experience. Leadership is about tough choices, depression, stress, calculations, hard work, smart work, celebrations, victories, and failures. If none of these things is appealing to you then you are not a leader.

You probably must be asking yourself whether leaders enjoy being depressed. The truth of the matter is, they don't but they know that it only lasts for a moment, and then it subsides. That is the spirit of a leader. Leaders never dwell on the bitter past but they sweeten the taste of the future. If you cannot be in a position to suffer the pain today so that people coming after you may enjoy the benefits of your actions then you are not a leader. Leaders know that they never live to enjoy the fruits of their actions. Those who enjoy their sweat are the beneficiaries whom they serve or the generation that comes after them.

Some of the leaders that I admire a lot include iconic figures like the late Nelson Mandela, Desmond Tutu, Martin Luther King Jr. inter alios. These are people who prophesied the sweetness of their action for the generation that was coming after them. We might not be there yet but they created a remarkable change in the lives of people. Leaders are those who take actions on behalf of others. They know that they create value that they do not have to enjoy. They put themselves on the front line ready to suffer so that innocent people can live at peace.

What then is leadership? Leadership is a pain and satisfaction story. It is a failure and success story. Leadership is the act of doing the impossible so that you can add importance to lives of the people whom you are serving. A leader is a servant.

One of the ways to inspire people under your leadership so that they can realize their true potentials is to do more yourself. How much pain can you handle before you tap out? Furthermore, how much pain can you handle in place of another person so that they can achieve freedom? Is that not what Jesus did? Servant leadership is leading like Christ. So many books talk about this and I am blowing the same trumpet. Just like the son of man gave his life to suffer a shameful death on the cross so is a leader supposed to act. Run away from leadership if you think you cannot cope with the criticisms and success that it brings. Run with leadership if you know that the good stays forever and failures only last for a moment.

To be a leader, you must not be all-knowing, however, you should be a person who can improvise, consult, and work with think tanks in decision making. Seventy percent of actions of leaders are things they make up on the spot. They are people who can extemporize a solution logically by studying it. This does not mean that their actions are right at all times but they boldly step into action knowing the possibilities of the outcome.

In every action you do, there are only two outcomes and so it is the same with decision making. It can either go wrong or right. If it goes wrong, then you can still turn things around and make the best out of your decisions. In case of the latter, then you can improve them to better standards. In everything you do, there is always room for improvement.If you choose to be a leader, step into action boldly and be in charge, ready to admit your mistakes and crown those who help you on your way to success.

On Jeopardizing Important Things

The happiness of your life depend on upon the quality of your thoughts: therefore guard accordingly and take care that you entertain no notions unsuitable to virtue and reasonable nature ~ Marcus Aurelius

Treat Entrepreneurship like a good pie: Don't waste it, know your limits, and never jeopardize important things. Take a break when necessary but remember to put in all the efforts and more if needed. A lot of people always want to be successful and from what they hear on the news, motivational speakers, giant investors, sharks and dragons, they are told that entrepreneurship is the only way to freedom. I challenge this stance by saying that that is not the case. Entrepreneurship is a jail that most people always want to opt out of.

Often times I speak to potential entrepreneurs who choose to pick my brain on challenges and successes I have seen on my way as an author, a founder, a director and an entrepreneur. My advice to them is; it really does not matter. My story is totally different from anybody else's. I hold a different history to anybody who thinks I am successful. First of all, success is not what I am going for therefore to view me as a successful entrepreneur is in itself wrong. I value happiness over success because there are successful people who have not attained the certainty of happiness; therefore their success becomes more of a curse to them.

To those who still think that they can make it in entrepreneurship, never jeopardize these three important things:

Vision

If you think you are going into entrepreneurship for freedom, fun and money then you are very wrong and you better look into working for other people. There is more freedom working for others than there is in starting your own business. You get to work from nine in the morning until five then you are set loose to do whatever you want. That is not the case with starting your own business. One of my retired board members told me as we were starting the organization not "to do it unless I could not do it."

To attain happiness by starting your own business, never focus on your product or service, focus on the needs of your customers. What is it that they lack that only you can help them attain? Business is about reality and remember your customers are too smart to be duped. This question can only be addressed when you focus on the vision of what your firm is going to carry out.

It is therefore imperative to write a vision statement before you start your business. A vision statement follows the problem identity and how long the problem is going to be. The vision statement should include the big picture of what your organization wants to achieve. Never forget to include a vision statement in anything you are doing.

Mission

Just as it is with the vision statement, a mission statement is very important when starting your own business. What is it that you are going to do to make sure that your vision becomes a reality? It is at this stage that most potential entrepreneurs quit because they think of the amount of work that lies ahead of them after they launch their business. Planning your mission is totally different from executing it therefore those who are scared by thinking of the amount of work that lies ahead of them are not fit to lead and or start their own business. In entrepreneurship, you either embrace the work you are getting yourself into or work for other people forever. Your mission statement will be your daily check to confirm that you are still operating within the confines of your original policies. Write a mission statement and again I say, write it.

Values

A lot of organizations, entrepreneurs and businesses choose to ignore the value statement. It is because of the values that you are going to add to the community that you are starting your organization. There are only two things involved in this case, you either add value or take away value, no mutually exclusive events. If your business is taking away value, be advised that it is short lived. Someone is thinking and now writing a business plan that will hit your business hard, trample on it and mash it into finer particles. You are a loser and still going to fail even more if you cannot think of adding value to the lives of your customers.

Reasons and Excuses

Negative thinking is subtle and deceptive. It wears many faces and hides behind the mask of excuses. It is important to strip away the mask and discover the real, root emotions ~ Robert Schuler

The biggest barrier to starting a company isn't ideas, funding or experience. It's excuses ~ Sara Lacy

There is a thin line separating reasons from excuses and often times people cross the line unknowingly. For mega success one ought to sharpen their thoughts and process of reasoning to build cogent and coherent premises that support their argument.

To attain mega success by reducing excuses and promoting reasons, one ought to:

Build Coherence

This is the precision and quality of being logical and consistent. It is always easy to fall into cheap fallacies that lead to lies and dishonesty when one defends his excuses especially after failure. It is then important to be truthful and tell a situation as it is.

Accepting Mistakes

Any moment you openly accept a mistake, you reduce the time it takes to solve the problem, you keep yourself away from excuses, and you create no room for lies. Naturally human beings, just like other animals, will defend themselves when they hear great danger approaching. Self-defense is our involuntary action and that is where we go wrong. We fail to understand that our brains tend to freeze and fail to multitask making us sound illogical with disjointed arguments.

Laugh at Your Mistakes

On my quest to meet 365 influential leaders in 365 days, I met with the president of a Christian University in Ontario and he was very open with me. One thing I learned with him among other leaders I met was that when he was telling me about his past mistakes, he was laughing at them.

It is important to do this first because it makes you own your mistakes. Secondly it makes you go above minor things that hold you down, and third it shows that you are open to change and to learn. That is how mega success is attained. It takes a while but one ought to try this.

Stay Calm

This is an action I prefer to call a power play. It works best in arguments, in bargaining, and in emergencies. Never lose it. Hold it tight even when it hurts. Any moment you lose control of your emotions, it will only show how irrelevant and careless you are. You can still defend your arguments without raising your voice.

Taking this stand will always make people apologize to you at the end even when you are the wrong one. Staying calm makes you take control of a demanding situation. This does not mean that mega successful people do not get angry. They do, but if you think you are not in a position to communicate then keep quiet. Ask for more time to process your thoughts and never approach any argument when you are mad.

Take Time

It is good to digest your thoughts and arguments. This way, you know what to say and what not to say and when to say it. Remember you are not in any argument to win but to learn, therefore take time to listen and be slow in responding.

Be Positive

Negative attitudes will only give you negative results making you a mega loser! Approach challenges with a positive mind. Never let your emotions control you but rather take charge of your emotions. Arguments or questions on one's failure should not rise to battleground and exchange of bitter words. Never let your ignorance show up where your intelligence is supposed to take charge.

On Going Big or Bigger

Do the things you fear to do and keep on doing it, that is the quickest and surest way ever yet discovered to conquer fear ~ Dale Carnegie.

We learn more by looking for an answer to a question and not finding it than we do from learning the answer itself ~ Lloyd Alexander.

The only failure we are sure of is the one we intentionally chose to abandon, so never, ever give up! Entrepreneurship and leadership are environments that can easily prune out the unfruitful branches. Never wait for nature to take its own course in your organization. You started it and you are the controller not nature. If you can resist nature from creeping into your business then you are a leader. Your business is going to do great despite all the market torrents that might toss your boat higher.

If you are reading this book and you are in this chapter, you should know that somebody saw value in bringing you forth in this world and carried you in their womb for a whole nine months. If they were to give up, you would not be here reading this book and thinking of starting your own business. Show your appreciation back to them by not giving up. As a man, I cannot fully grasp the feeling of bearing a child but from what I hear our beloved mothers out there say, it is the most difficult, painful and tiring task.

Why start a business if you know you are going to quit? Why rise and fail to shine? The sun may rise in the morning but get covered with clouds, mists and fog but that does not mean that it is not shining. Go behind the covered sky and watch it shine in its whole radiance. You might go through the worst in your business, and the fact is, you will go through some really rough times, but those challenges should not affect your enthusiasm.

Some people fear to venture into entrepreneurship with the fact that they do not want to lose all they have. Well and good, continue reserving the little you have but you are missing out on great opportunities to grow as an individual. Everything comes and goes and as I am writing this book, I do not know about my next second.

Since life is such a flower that blooms and fades away in the evening, it is better to use it to do greater things while we can. You have come too far to lose. Never give up.

On Developing an Urgency of Doing

It isn't enough to poses wisdom, you should use it too ~ Cicero.

I have been impressed with the urgency of doing, knowing is not enough; we must apply. Being willing is not enough, we must do ~ Leonardo da Vinci.

Without a sense of urgency, desire loses its value ~ Jim Rohn.

Of all the gifts that we have in this world, nothing is more valuable than time. Therefore, we should spend our time wisely. The only time we have in our hand is the present; it makes more sense to spend our present moments doing useful things, adding value to our lives or the lives of those we are serving. In every objective you have set, always develop an urgency of doing.

Everything is achievable if well planned, but it does not only stop at planning. The execution ranks top after planning. It is easy to stop a project in the middle because of the psychological effects of planning. There is always a feeling of accomplishments after planning and before implementing, yet the heavy load lies in the execution part. This could only be happening to me alone, but have you planned something and before you do it, you feel like it is already done? Our minds can trick our feelings and take away the urgency of doing, making us lapse in executing our duties. Therefore to beat the urgency of doing, one ought to:

Plan in Advance

Planning in advance gives you a leeway on what comes after the other. In my first book Strategies of Entrepreneurial Leadership, I talk about planning as the best way to spend our time. One should always plan their day prior to retiring at night. Take the last 15 minutes of your day before you go to bed and figure out what needs to be done and how to get these tasks done in the day that follows.

When planning your day, take away those personal activities that consume your work time and plot them on a different schedule. I always take the first 30 minutes when I wake up every day to catch up with global news, read personal emails and plan my work emails when I arrive in the office. I also take another 30 minutes responding to work emails then go straight to what my errands for the day are. The other time when I have to check my emails are during breaks and lunchtime. In between it is accomplishing all the tasks I have on my desk. Setting your work time and personal time is important because you do not want to mix your work time with family or personal time. Do what needs to be done and make sure you do it within the first five seconds you think of it to avert procrastination.

On Dealing with People,

Education begins the gentleman, but reading, good company and reflection must finish him ~ John Locke

Those not chasing their dreams should stay out of the way of those who are ~ Tim Fargo

Entrepreneurship is about dealing with people. Treat all equal and give them the best. They define you. Entrepreneurship is a road taken by few and a big percentage of those few also fail miserably. In entrepreneurship or any leadership position, failing is the only thing guaranteed. For success, you must be ready to work. This demands that you have the right team to work with.

Some people just like to make easy things seem impossible, get rid of them. Birds of the same feathers flock together. This is probably one of the most undervalued statements of all times. Look around you and count up to four of your closest friends. These are the people you hang out with and have fun with when you are free.

Do these people believe in you? Do they believe in your efforts? Do they believe you can make it as a leader or as an entrepreneur? There are some people we entertain in our lives yet they cause more damage to us than good. Starting a business is so hard and stressful that it is wise to spend your time with either other business people or people who are successful in it.

Of course this is not how society should be, but we either decide to sacrifice our time for the success of our business or entertain every Tom, Dick and Harry that we meet. If you are honest with yourself, you will find it more beneficial to be with people who add value in your life than those who take value away from it.

It requires wisdom to discern who to be with. If your mindset is to success and happiness, then there will be tropism towards achievers. They should be your external stimuli to do more, dream more, and value more. This is the time, do not wait. If possible, do not even finish reading this chapter, prune people who always attract you to negative things and get close to those who have a mindset of success and happiness.

Failure is not enough reason not to try doing greater things. If birds of the same feathers really flock together, then why are you with people who do not change you for the best? I have been meeting a lot of business leaders and investors who are successful and endeavouring to learn what makes them successful. One of the things that they all agree on is hard and smart work and being with good company. Your group defines who you are so stop wasting your time with people who have no dreams. The fact that somebody cannot dream big should not infiltrate in your mind. You coin your own destiny. Be smart.

On Thinking Differently

The voice of intellect is a soft one but it does not rest until it has gained a hearing ~ Sigmund Freud.

Two qualities are dispensable: first an intellect that, even the darkest hour, retains some glimmering of the inner light which leads to truth; and second, the courage to follow this faint light wherever it may lead ~ Carl von Clausewitz

A leader is anyone who believes deep down in their hearts that they are destined to do great things. Why think if you have nothing better to think about? Society has made us understand and agree with numbers. This is not to challenge statistics. Statistics is one of the true ways of understanding our world until it is doctored then it fails to accomplish its mission. Since leaders are philosophers and philosophers are thinkers, think differently.

All along, I have been highly against big numbers and I like listening to both parties and pay attention to the underdogs. It always raises my conscience when multitudes are for an idea. Why would I not want to think differently? It is easy to get trapped in the torrents of the mass following and get swept away by the kinetic energy of numbers. But sometimes numbers are not enough.

God blessed us with minds so that we can think. Everyone has an obligation to reason and we can choose to use our minds or fail to use them. The decision is yours. One thing I do not like is to conform to the norms of society. If only people could ask "why?" then we could make the world a better place to be in.

How many times have we been lied to by politicians and we still endorse them for more than one term in office? This is just one piece of evidence of how humanity has refused to use the gift of reasoning. Companies reason for us and we respond by flocking to their stores shopping for those things we think are good for us yet we fail to ask "why?"

A leader is one who sees things differently and questions the normal practices in our daily lives. Entrepreneurs who fail to ask themselves "why" go wrong. Why would I start a new business? Why come up with a new idea yet the world seems to be moving well with all the ideas that are helping shape it at the current time? Above all, why think?

We always drum up the support for change yet we fail to understand why we need change. We generate new business ideas and we fail to ask why we need new businesses. One of the problems that our leaders have lied to us about is democracy. My gospel is; if you have brain, then you have no reason not to think.

One of the reasons why I like challenging the status quo is to understand how many people, governed by rules and laws of this world, understand what those laws are. People become successful because they fail to abide by rules or simply ignore them. As a leader, you should ask yourself why you are not challenging the status quo and again do not just challenge the status quo because you want to cause trouble. You are blessed with a brain to use wisely not to waste your thoughts on things that add no value to people's lives. Feel free to think, it is not a sin. Most people fear status-quo but they do not respect it. It is better to understand it before you even respect it.

On the Pursuit of Happiness

We hold these truths to be self-evident: that all men are created equal, that they are endowed by their Creator with certain unalienable rights; that among these are, life liberty and the pursuit of happiness ~ Thomas Jefferson.

Happiness is the meaning and purpose of life, the whole aim and end of human existence ~ Aristotle

When a thoughtful human being has overcome incentives to vice and is aware of having done his bitter duty, he finds himself in a state that could be called happiness, a state of contentment and peace of mind in which virtue is its own reward ~ Emmanuel Kant.

Unlike the philosophical debates on the meaning of pursuit of happiness, how it applies in our society today and the ethics behind it, this book covers pursuit of happiness solely for its business reasons and how it can help entrepreneurs and leaders achieve their maximum success, which they are working towards.

Aristotle can be credited as the father of pursuit of happiness. He considered this a branch of science that solely depended on an individual. Aristotle was a student of Plato who studied under Socrates and had influenced the modern philosophy by his contribution to mathematics, physics, logic and agriculture.

It is reasonable to say that both men and women always work towards attaining self-sufficiency or rather those things that make them happy. People go to work to make money so that they can live happily. Some go to church because they believe that God is the source of all happiness, some work on building their character believing that it is the source of happiness.

Some people engage in different activities to build a reputation, pride and other self-fulfilling wishes. But the main reason for doing this is to be happy. Just as a pilot enjoys flying through the skies above, just as a surgeon gets excited after a successful operation, just as captain feels good after sailing the seas, so is a leader or an entrepreneur after a breakthrough.

A few people land in professions they do not enjoy and business leadership is one of those positions that you cannot just wake up to find yourself in. Not to say that it has fewer frustrations. Business people are some of the most frustrated people on earth but that never stops them from going for their dreams. One engineer once told me that "those who think it is impossible should get out of the way of those who believe it is possible."

As is with any debate, there are always antagonists and protagonists, those against an idea and those who hold it firmly and do not want to lose it. Therefore, in this chapter we are going to discuss, what is crucial; happiness or success?

Some of the debates, comments and answers I got from over 100,000 followers on twitter on this topic were that success and happiness are complimentary; success is the most important thing, while others believed that happiness was the only thing that people should go for. Can we consider the pursuit of happiness a success of its own kind? In my opinion, a continuous pursuit of happiness is more important than a strong desire to succeed. What is it that you find joy in and you value so much that you never get bored doing it over and over again?

How many people do we know who were once successful, (whatever your definition of success is) but today are going through tough life? So is success all that is? For what is a man who has not been taught what to do with success after attaining it? These achievements can lead to frustrations and boredom of the highest order.

The lexical meaning of success is the accomplishment of an aim or purpose. Happiness is defined as a mental and emotional state of well-being, characterized by positive or pleasant emotions ranging from contentment to intense joy. Is it therefore good to be happy or successful?

Albert Einstein a theoretical physicist once said, "Try not to become a man of success, but rather a man of value." If what makes you happy is creating value either in your life or in other people's, then you are headed in the right direction. It is very rare to be successful without failing. Does that mean that we have to quit after a few attempts? If we make the pursuit of happiness our ultimate goal, then no matter how many failures we go through, we will still be able to rejoice knowing that there is that one moment when we will be happy and it does not stop at success only.

Those who never succeed always consider success greatest. For any moment you attain a prize, you will realize that there is more to be done to maintain that rank. After all why would Olympians try to break their own records? Some of the fastest Olympians alive on earth keep working hard towards beating their own records. Why? Because all they need is happiness not success. They have already been successful by breaking world records. It does not solely stop at being the best.

A purposeful living consists of incessant desire of happiness that can only be attained through hard work. Just as Benjamin Franklin, a scientist and a writer once said, "Happiness consists more in small conveniences of pleasures that occur every day, than in great pieces of good fortune, that happen but seldom."

Happiness therefore, underwrites a greater drive of all beings. The entire purpose and end of human's actuality should be planted in happiness.

On Leaders and Visionary Leaders

A leader has the vision and conviction that a dream can be achieved, he inspires the power and energy to get it done ~ Ralph Lauren.

Where there is no vision, the people perish ~ Proverbs 29:18

The greatest danger for most of us is not that our aims are too high and we miss it, but that it is too low and we reach it ~ Michelangelo

There is a great demand for good leadership. Good leadership is the scarcest resource the world has experienced in years. What I mean by good leadership is visionary leadership. Anybody can be a leader but not all are visionary leaders. The world is fed up with leaders and it is now in deep hunger and thirst for visionary leaders.

Visionary leaders are like armed prophets. They have a reason to make people follow them. They are game changers and they can communicate the big picture in the simplest way possible. When they speak, they connect their visions to a real life experience. They focus on adding value to people's lives.

If you are a Christian then you are probably familiar with some visionary leaders and the themes of their leadership. Abraham led because he was the father of all nations. He knew that God was going to use him to fill the earth. When God told him that his descendants were going to be like the sand on the shore of the sea or like stars in the sky at night, he believed it and acted on the vision. That was his guiding message in everything he did. "I will surely bless you, and I will surely multiply your offspring as the stars of heaven and as the sand that is on the seashore." (Genesis 22:17, ESV).

Moses was another visionary leader with a message to take God's children to the Promised Land. Canaan was a land full of milk and honey which we still value to this day. Moses used this vision from God to lead his people but only under a condition that those who obeyed God and kept his commandments were to inherit that beautiful land flowing with gems.

The great need of visionary leadership is everywhere. Countries and nations are looking for politicians with visions to improve and grow economies. Very few live to see that vision of improved development come true. Businesses are in high demand of visionary CEOs, but there are quite a few visionary CEOs out there. Churches are in high demand of visionary leaders, those who can engage the community, bring new believers into the church and cultivate strong spiritual foundations to new converts but there is only a handful of them out there. So what makes visionary leadership be in high demand?

Sacrifice

Visionary leaders fully give their lives for the course determined by their followers. They endure the pain and get the worst hitting. They are always on the front line in times of challenge when they are needed the most. They never gave in to false beliefs of impossibilities. To them everything is possible.

Persistence

Visionary leaders only rest when they have achieved their dreams. They work towards the broader perspective and it does not matter to them how many times they slip, fall and get back up. They never believe in staying on the ground once they fall. They rise and shine for it makes no sense to them why one would rise and fail to shine.

Tenacity

Visionary leaders are determined and they know their direction. They have the ability to grip on to their vision until it comes true. They understand that just as you approach victory that is when the worst happens. They never give up when all hope seems gone. They understand that pain only lasts for a moment then it fades away.

Hope

Visionary leaders are hopeful people. They know that as long as they are alive, they can achieve anything. They build unity and form organization synergies to push them forward. Above all, they understand that nobody can push them forward other than themselves. They strive towards success but they never stop and dwell on their achievements. They look at victory as a point to stop and take a breath before they start climbing another mountain. They know that life is what you make it be and if you have faith in God then you can do anything you set your mind on.

Visionary leaders are the ones that the world is craving for. To be a visionary leader, one ought to understand the needs of the people and one must be ready to risk it all to offer the best solution that the world needs.

On Slaying the Dragon

If you know the enemy and you know yourself, you need not fear the results of a hundred battles ~ Sun Tzu

The first duty of man is to conquer fear; he must get rid of it, he cannot act till then ~ Thomas Carlyle.

To him who is in fear, everything rustles ~ Sophocles

The biggest challenge that most entrepreneurs and other leaders go through is fear. Fear is a dragon, it can consume you in no time, it is scary, and looks like a giant. It can kill you before your time and it can hinder you from success despite the potentials you have of blowing the competition out of the water. Fear always comes in two forms; the fear of success and the fear of failure. The former can be worst and devastating while the latter is equally as bad and can hinder you from freely expressing your potentials. The question we need to ask ourselves is "how do we slay this dragon?" It does not matter what form of fear it is, what is important is growing out of it, which can be achieved by doing the following.

Avoiding Cynics

Some people, and surprisingly a lot of them, will forever doubt your potentials. What you need to do is to repel them with facts and works. They are not worth your time so why pay attention to them? They will reduce you to a tiny particle and blow you away like dust.

One thing you need to know is that you are already in motion. You are reading this book because you are a snowball rolling down from a mountain, ready to cause an avalanche. Sweep away the sceptics before they wipe you out. They will show you how much you do not know, how weak you are, how uneducated you are and how useless your efforts are. Never believe them. Believe in yourself and understand that we all have our own weaknesses. The fact that you have a mindset of running your own business or leading a people puts you in a better position to succeed in life because you are a thinker. Soon enough, you will be hiring your doubters to work for you. It is just a matter of time. Never give up.

Do Not Let Age Deter You

This mostly affects young ambitious leaders and entrepreneurs. People will rule you out because of your age but they fail to consider the solutions you have to offer. It does not matter whether you are tall, short, skinny, big, young or old. If you can reason well, use logic appropriately and see ahead, then nobody should stand in your way. Never listen to people talking behind your back. They were not meant to be in front so let them stay right there at the back. After all, you lead, they follow.

Know the Dragon

You cannot fight a war that you do not know. Each and every one of us has our own dragons to slay. As I have mentioned in earlier chapters and in a number of my other literatures that failure is the only thing guaranteed in this world. We should not fear failure because it does not need any effort to fail. It is the only easiest thing to achieve in life. Know your fears and build a plan to overcome them. Courage becomes a strong weapon to fight your dragon.

Be Strong and Very Courageous

Courage does not mean you do not fear anything. It simply means you have your weaknesses and fears but you take a bold step to face them. We were born once, we live once and die once so why not be adventurous and try to be courageous at least once? After all, we do not want to be trampled upon by every single challenge we meet on our way. Go out there and try doing new things. Success favours risk takers so if you cannot take the risk to use the weapons you hold in hand to slay the dragon in front of you, you will live a miserable life until you get in your grave. Why live in regrets if you had the opportunities to try? Trying is always better than not trying.

Act Out in Faith

Do it big, we do not have time to act small. When you are going to war, prepare to conquer kingdoms, set captive your opponents and above all act in faith. Believe that with God, you can do everything. We are blessed with wisdom and God's protection and love. Just believe that you can do it and when you do, do it real big!

On Moving Backward

It is easier to find men who will volunteer to die than to find those who are willing to endure pain with patience ~ Julius Caesar.

I assess the power of a will by how much resistance, pain, torture it endures and knows how to turn to its advantage ~ Friedrich Nietzsche.

A lot of things in motion started from going backwards. Think of a person shooting arrows from a bow, they first have to pull it backwards. Think of a person firing a gun at a target, the trigger moves backward. How about a soccer player going to take a penalty shot? They first have to move backward to gain the momentum to hit the ball.

A lot of things in this world involve going backward before you move to success.

Nobody puts a ladder parallel against the wall to climb to the top. They have to move the ladder backwards so that they can be stable and reduce the workload of climbing and for stability. To lead, you first have to be led. Learn, make mistakes and then emerge victoriously. However, most of us always want to take the shortcut to the top. We fail to recognize the importance of moving backwards.

To gain dividends and/or build a profit margin, first you have to part with money in the form of capital. Money does not come unless you invest which means moving backwards. Successful and happy investors understand this principle while most people always ignore it. Literally, it makes sense to move from zero to something however that is not the reality. Good things just never come.

A bigger percentage of people in developed nations believe that they will win the lottery at some point in their life. Now to win a lottery, you have to purchase the raffle tickets. This in return reduces your assets because they are expenditures. The possibilities of winning now become probable but you stand higher chances of winning by purchasing a lot of lottery tickets.

Leadership of any sort has a lot of backward motion. Great leaders understand that the end is good and if it is not good yet, then it is yet to come. Therefore they:

Never Lose Hope

Hope is the belief that everything is possible before you achieve or attain your goals. Hope can take you where no car, airplane, train, or person can take you. Hope can keep you alive with a great promise that the pain and backward motion you are taking or going through will end and that you are going to get a projectile shot towards greatness. Most successful and great leaders bear the pains and losses of backward motion with a clear understanding that this is where it all starts. It is hope that keeps them alive.

Never Stop Believing

To believe is to strongly have faith in something. The last thing I expect from anybody I coach is not to believe in themselves. I believe that if you have your mindset to do greater things and you have faith in your potential then nothing and nobody can stand in your way. You can never lose what you don't have therefore try and set your mind that you can achieve anything. Everything is possible and for some of us who are believers already know that with God everything is possible. You can achieve everything through Christ who strengthens you.

Never Lose Vision

Vision is the broader depiction, the end product seen from a distance. The product is always very vivid in mind before it is attained and it is that mirage that we see and have hope in that drives us towards changing them into reality. Our ideas are the most worthless things we own if we do not turn them into action. The only way to make a dream come true is to wake up. Dreamers are slumbers and nobody acts when asleep. Vision is like building a sand castle by the beach. A strong wind or a tidal wave can easily sweep it away. If you want a castle then build the real one. Do not run to the beach and make one in the sand and start shouting and dancing of how magnificent your work is. That is an ineffectual vision.

Never Take the Short Route

Shortcut routes yield to no long term success. It is a route taken by the lazy, those who are quick to discourage and slow to act. They never say anything important but useless talks that kill vision. Sadly you might be one of them but it is never too late to change. Change now! If you are not under this category, then you are a leader, a pioneer of success. You understand hard work and I bet your top five friends are hard workers too. Shortcuts will cut you short, therefore short change them before they short change you.

Never Take No for an Answer

"No" is for losers and the hopeless without direction. Those who wait for others to approve everything they want to do never think for themselves and are slaves to fear. They have been held captive by negativity and they fail to realize how important they are. They never see their true potential. Leaders never take 'No' for an answer. They distance themselves from neigh Sayers.

Leaders and great entrepreneurs are the real daredevils. They plunge into the ocean of leadership without worrying about the dangers of the coral reefs. They never fear the alligators waiting for them in the water with their mouths wide open. They never dodge the attacks thrown at them just to test if they are fake or real. That is true leadership. Leaders are restless, they never believe in making same mistake over and over again. They view the world differently and from their crazy perspectives, the world has grown to become better than what it was yesterday. Never take 'no' for an answer.

Never Appreciated at the Onset

Leaders and those who believe in change speak their mind and are always rejected at first. The Greek philosopher Socrates, the father of modern philosophy was highly rejected and condemned to death. Baruch Espinoza, the father of atheism was rejected, expelled, cursed and excommunicated from Church. Jesus was crucified on the cross simply because he called himself Messiah. One thing that these great people share in common is that their ideas are still being experienced in our modern society to date.

I wrote my first book *Strategies of Entrepreneurial Leadership* when I was in university. I was broke, in debt, and nearly homeless. Those whom I approached to write a "Forward" page for me rejected it citing grammatical errors, lack of structure, spelling mistakes, lack of experience, and lack of solid transforming stories to share. Some whom I used as examples went as far as ordering me to delete their names from the book which I did. Let nobody determine your destiny for you. Evaluate what they say and if there are things you need to adjust on, then act on them. Understand that you will be rejected. You will be despised especially when you start at an early age. Today, people are posting and reposting my quotes on social media from the same book that was once rejected. Never take the attacks that people throw at you personally. Take them with a grain of salt. Cynics hold no spot on your way to success. Attack them with meekness but work hard and smart to prove them wrong. Be an undercurrent, sweep the floors of the ocean from beneath the water and explode into a Tsunami when it is already too late to be under anybody's control.

Never Become Predictable

Great leaders attack when they are least expected to. Successful entrepreneurs launch new products when their rivals do not expect them to. They hit hard, they leave people dazed and wondering what has happened. Of all the things, nobody should predict your moves.

The first presidential debate between Mitt Romney and Barack Obama is a great example. Obama was almost tongue-tied to see Mitt attack him one point after the other. Little did Romney know that this was a strategy to be used against him in their second and last debate. Obama came back swinging high and hard-throwing attacks to every single plan that Mitt Romney had. In the end, U.S.A said yes to Obama for the second time. Plan your actions and let nobody understand your movements. Be unpredictable and hit with high results. In every success you make, celebrate after calculating your next victory. Your enemies are strategizing as you celebrate therefore get ready for another attack. That is the importance of planning and being unpredictable. People will always pull you back, never give up, and go for your vision boldly.

On Finishing Your Competitors

I have been up against tough competition all my life. I wouldn't know how to get along without it ~ Walt Disney.

The best revenge is not to be like your enemy ~ Marcus Aurelius.

There is nothing to benefit from by completely finishing your competitors. Monopoly is for cowards, the self-centred and those who are weak and cannot handle challenges. It is a step taken by people who like authority but what is so good in monopoly that everyone today wants to solely rule the market? Never totally and completely finish your rivals; they are the ones to crown you on your way to glory.

Frugality is not wrong but being too frugal can be an easy way of diminishing yourself from this beautiful world. It is only through competition that nature can best select the fit for the market. Any moment you give your rival a chance to live, you are giving people a show to watch. A victory hard won is sweeter than an easy come victory. As you fight, remember to hurt your enemies but always give them a second chance to tell your story of how terrifying you are. However, you should always remember to:

Stay ahead

Never let your enemy come too close to your position. Always remember that some people like to support the underdogs so never humiliate your opponent. You will lose sympathy supporters that way. You always want to make your market struggle as theatrics for your fans. They should see each and every movement you take as a hard-won battle. Nothing makes your fans happier than to see that through their support victory is won. As much as you want to stay ahead, never win over your rival by greater margins. Beat them but remember never to humiliate them.

Start a New Rivalry if Necessary

Sometimes you do not want direct confrontation so that you can secure your reputation. In such cases, it is better to start new companies without your key enemy knowing and let the new company attack your rival directly. As it is with any fight, your rival will change tactics towards facing your opponent. Use that time to sit back, relax and watch them fight. This way, you get more time to develop new strategies, new technology hence putting yourself above the two fighting bulls.

Creating new rivalry also elevates you to a master's level. Anybody who wants to fight you must first confront the small threats you planted before they get to the master. This is one way of shielding yourself from unnecessary attacks. You are the master, craft your moves.

Never Leak Out Your Secrets

You are in a battleground; you do not want to be vulnerable. Never play at your rivals mercies. To be called a master, you must operate on a different philosophy than anybody else. Be a scarecrow but remember that scarecrows are often times dead and can cause no harm so it is better to show action to confirm to your enemies that you are alive. Keep your secrets water tight, never be arrogant. By concealing your intentions, you become unpredictable. Being secretive gives you mileage above all your enemies. How can you be a master if everybody has mastered your skills? Be enigmatic and act with boldness.

Say No to Mergers

People who see you as a threat will lure you with goodies. They will set a trap and try to catch you. Remember at this stage of success, some people will set bait for you and once you insert your head in the trap, you are dead. You are gone. You are history never to be heard of again. Say no, practise no and believe in no. Once you sign a deal, all your powers are gone and nobody will remember you. Instead of being the master and making people dance to your tunes, you will be dancing to other people's tunes. Since they already know and understand you as a threat in the market, they will finish you. They will maim you and suffocate your business. They are ready to assimilate you and your company. Say no unless the agreement favours you.

Control Your Emotions

You are on a battlefield, and you are going to get hurt. Leadership is not a place of beauty. It is not a place to sit pretty. Flowers are beautiful, puppies are cute, sunsets are awesome but leadership is awful, it is scary, it is a monster that everybody wants to attack. With leadership comes emotions but learn that some attacks are tackled logically rather than emotionally. Differentiate each problem and know how to attack them. The truth is, you are going to be hurt by your followers, employees, board members and your enemies. Master the art of emotional control and never let it control you. You are the master not your emotions.

Compete

The best way to deal with competition is to show up for the race, take the lap in your stride without copying anybody's pace. Learn to be yourself. Let your actions enhance your image. You are better off being you than anybody else.

On Management and Leadership

I suppose leadership at one time meant muscles; but today it means getting along with people ~ Mahatma Gandhi.

Leadership is diving for a loose ball, getting the crowd involved, getting other players involved. It's being able to take it as well as dish it out. That is the only way you are going to get respect from the players ~ Larry Bird.

When it is obvious that the goals cannot be reached, don't adjust the goals, adjust the action steps ~ Confucius.

Plato believed that kings were the only people who understood justice because they were the only people who grasped the philosophical concepts of leadership. In the world today, division and specialization of labour have made it easy for people to focus only on one area and see success. We therefore ask ourselves, what is the difference between managers and leaders?

Leaders are those who inspire others to achieve the visions that impact and change lives for the better through a way of projecting expertise that assures confidence in the hearts and minds of those who follow them. Managers are those who coordinate, organize, command, plan and support the executions that turn visions into reality.

It is possible for a leader to be a manager but managers do not often make good leaders, and good leaders do not make good managers. When a business or any organization is starting, vision, mission, and value statements are written. This part is always played by the leaders. They are the ones who ask; "what is it that we can do to improve the standards of living of people either through daily experience or totally eradicating a problem?" After answering this question, the matter is then transferred to the managers.

The key role of managers is to concentrate on the mission statement. A mission statement is a formal summary of the aims and guidelines of an organization. It highlights in brief, what must be done to make the vision become true. It is the manager's task to implement using these guidelines within the organization's peripheries to ensure satisfying results to leaders and people being served by the organization.

To make it more understandable, this is the simplified version of the subject and who it affects/responsible.
  a) Vision of the organization ----- Implemented by a leader
  b) Mission of the organization---- Implemented by a manager
  c) Value of the organization------- Affects people served by the organization.

Leaders are the overseers of the entire organization while managers are the implementers of the dreams. It takes a lot of work for both managers and leaders to build a team synergy. One of the traits that are highly required to make this goal a possibility is patience. Even though you want to be patient, a successful leader understands the urgency of implementation. Once a decision is made or a great idea clicks in their mind, it must be implemented forthwith.

An organization with great chemistry between the manager and the leader is destined to succeed. Wisdom plays a pivotal role in such a scenario and it needs in-depth understanding of the leadership philosophy. Leadership and management have one thing in common, though, they both need good decision makers. People who understand the risks involved in every step of their action and must be willing to move on in the case of any failure. Great leaders inspire ordinary people to do extraordinary things.

The Art of Delegation

Delegating means letting others become the experts and hence the best ~ Timothy Firnstahl.

The great leaders are like the best conductors, they reach beyond the notes to reach the magic in the players ~ Blaine Lee.

The art of delegation is something that every leader and entrepreneur need to master. It might sound easy but it is more complex than it sounds. Delegation is the art of spreading mundane tasks to people who can do them more cheaply, effectively and skillfully than the master can. It needs a lot of planning because delegation can either lead to your great breakthrough or great failure.

In my definition, I described delegation as an "art" that needs creativity, patience and skills. To paint a beautiful picture, you need the right brush, paint and skills and so is a delegation to success. For one to be great in delegating tasks, it is important to understand that:

You Don't Know

Socrates believed that he was the wisest of all the wise men because he knew what he did not know. To know what you know not makes you recognize that there are greater minds out there than you and if you tap into those skills, you can transform your efforts into mega success.

In our organization Succeed Africa and on my personal platform and website, I use a lot of external ideas to help me build a satisfying product for my customers. It does not make sense for me to spend an entire week designing a personal website if there are skilled people who can do it in a day or two.

Delegation Leads to Mega Success

If you have five tasks that need to be done, delegating three of them and having two that are very important, and that you can do very well reduces your time, resources and overhead it takes to get all the work done. Every leader and entrepreneur should learn how to maximize the utility of all the resources they have.

Time Waits for No Man

In my past literature, I have mentioned so many times that the underutilized and most abused resource we have is time. How you use your time determines the rate of returns you are going to get per output effort. The best way to wisely utilize your time is widely discussed in my first book *Strategies of Entrepreneurial Leadership*.

Outsourcing Can Save You a Fortune

This is something I have widely used and will continue to use. The best way to appreciate globalization is to delegate your mundane tasks to people who can leverage the work for you at a better rate. I am connected to most of the people who outsource for me through social media. Outsourcing has made me find an obedient and honest team to work with online. It is important for me to say that when you decide to go with outsourcing, please never exploit your team by paying them unworthy wages. Be kind and know that you are dealing with people with needs. After all what does it benefit us to gain the whole world with terrible reputation? Outsource with dignity.

Manage Wisely

Some people like to micro-manage, I don't. Anytime I am micro-managing a team of over 10 people, I am wasting important time that I can invest in developing the business. When hiring an employee to take over other duties from you, hire the best and let them have fun with everything they do. However it is not wrong to send a quick email or a brief phone call asking how they are doing, if they are meeting any challenges and how you can be of help.

On the Dual Existence Principle

The world has no gray zone. Phenomena always come in two. This is what I call the duo existence principle. It states that there is always an opposing side or object to everything that exists. Therefore there can only be good or bad, right or wrong, and one cannot be both all in and out at the same time.

Duo existence principle exists in corporate world as well. One is either a leader or a follower but cannot be both all at the same time. It is important that these two classes be familiar with the roles they play in a community otherwise there will be chaos.

For a harmonized operation and smooth running of everything we do, leaders must be obedient to their roles as well as their followers. It is the leader's actions that determine what his or her followers are going to do. Take a scenario where there is civil disobedience. People protest because they are not satisfied with the actions of their leaders.

Because success has no limits, men and women should always try to go past and beyond their goals. To stop from achieving more after your breakthrough is the easiest way to get back to failure especially if you still have the potential to go an extra mile.

Scales of Success and Failure

One can either fail to infinity or succeed to infinity. It depends on your mindset. This does not mean greed or laziness. There are more things that the world still needs to improve on, too much to be done to give success a limit.

What it Takes to Succeed or Fail

Failure is the only thing that does not require work. You just need to sit, do nothing and fail. Now there are also some people who try but get it wrong. Those, according to me, are not failures, they are people who miss the target but put forth at least some effort.

I have missed so many points in life. I missed a point on a course in the university; I missed a point on a business I started a while ago. I have missed points on employment opportunities. It is all about missing points! But what makes one successful is when you realize that missing a point is part of the equation to success. Success comes with hard work, resilience and staying true to your goals.

Intentionality

If you are not living intentionally to succeed, then you are living intentionally to fail. The intentionality builds resilience which most people always ignore. It does not matter what ideas you generate. You can be the smartest man or woman with an intelligent quotient greater than Einstein, but if you are not implementing your thoughts, then you are the most unavailing person to ever wander on the surface of the earth. In every thought you build, you must act on it. If you are not ready to fail, you are not ready to learn.

On Business the Jesus Way

Go therefore and make disciples of all nations~ Matthew 28:19

Trade is a name that is heavily used in the Bible. In the early days, it was done through the exchange of goods for goods. This switched to use of currency with a value equivalent to the utility of the product being traded. The use of money also promoted gold as a backup commodity for liquid money in economy. What is business the Jesus way?

In a Market Setting.

Markets were places where traders gathered to sell their products. Consumers would then go to find the right sellers with the right commodity they wanted. It was the responsibility of the consumers to search for what they wanted.

Prophets, kings, leaders, judges and inspired men of God used to gather people together, calling them to be part of an action or to honor and glorify God. Psalm 66 is a good example of this. The psalm who is representing the house of Israel is summoning other nations to come and witness and be part of what God had done.

Throughout the Old Testament, people are called, invitations are sent, and messengers were always on the go to bring people to be witnesses.

The Jesus Way

There is a paradigm shift on evangelism in the New Testament. Jesus, before ascending back to heaven after his death, commissioned his disciples to go. "Go ye and make disciples". Instead of inviting them to join him, Jesus advised them to get out of their comfort zones and go to the people.

It is not unusual to see businesses today going out to the people. Politician's campaigns involve meeting people in their hometowns and/or villages. Leaders go to the people. The church is going out to share the love of God with the world and so are the businesses. Consumers are there but producers must go to them.

This is the reason why major companies such as Google, Amazon, inter alia are walking away from their comfort zones. They have learned to become disciples. When I was starting our International organization, I went door to door, told people our story and shared it with almost everybody I knew.

Power of Business Discipleship

Business discipleship is all you need to learn. Go out to people. Customers are there, followers are waiting, supporters are keenly listening, just go. Go out and make people believers. If there are people who still do not know you, your vision and mission, know that they are your potential supporters. Tell the world in all ways possible of what you are doing. Just as Jesus sent out his disciples to go tell it to the world, you should also send your marketers, campaign teams, messengers to the people. Never keep quiet with a brilliant idea. You never know, maybe the world is waiting for you to change it for the better. Adopt the Jesus way. Go to people.

On Wealth, Poverty and Power

Power corrupts and absolute power corrupts absolutely ~ Lord Acton

Because power corrupts, society's demands for moral authority and character increase as the importance of the position increase ~ John Adams.

We should hold each other accountable in terms of wealth generation. Economics have explained in depth the scarcity of resources but in my opinion, there is nothing like scarcity of resources. The only scarce resource we have is time. Anybody can achieve, gain and gather as much wealth as he or she can work hard to get. I have read magazines, books and stories of self-made billionaires. It is true. So what do people need to become wealthy?

Mindset

All a person needs to be successful is the mindset of success. You can never have a hundred dollars if you do not have a plan to get a hundred dollars. You can never get a thousand dollars if you do not think of it. If you keep thinking and arguing about minimum wage all the time, that is where you will stay. You will live in abject poverty and you will not live a life to its fullest. I am not trying to materialize the life we live but why have limits when you can live a limitless life?

Plan

You can never have a thousand dollars with a hundred dollar plan. It will never work. One needs a strong plan to be successful. When writing your plan, focus on the goal. What is it that you want to achieve? Nobody writes a plan of what he or she already have, you plan ahead for things, things you have never achieved, things beyond your limits. Why have small plans when you can plan big?

Strategy

The name of the game is strategy. It will make you a winner or a serial loser. Strategy is the system that must be implemented, and how it is to be implemented to yield positive results really counts. Strategy differentiates you from any other person out there. You are unique and differently coded from anybody else. And if you don't know that you are differently coded, check your fingerprints and what they can be used for. The point is, you are already too unique and special in your own way, so why copy other people? Be creative or get out of the game.

Stinginess

It is good to be economical but foolish to be stingy. To get wealthy, you have to be prepared to invest. Our blessings can only be blessings if we use them to bless others. So why be stingy? Give and it shall come back to you. There are legitimate charities that need help, there are churches you can tithe to, and there are families on the streets that need assistance. And you still want to be stingy? Shame on you! We are blessed to bless.

On Poverty

Of all the things on the face of earth and heavens above, there is nothing as easy as failing. You do not even need to set your mindset to failure mode. Just fail. Success takes work; failure takes sleep, sitting, and doing nothing. Poverty is an undefined term as poor people in one country, economy and continent could be the middle class of another country. Even politics has failed to define poverty. Poverty does not exist. I was nearly homeless when I was starting my businesses, found myself sleeping on our office couch for a prime number of days in a week yet I looked at my monthly expenses and it was still over two hundred dollars. That is when I changed and made up my mind never to be economically challenged. From that day I have put in the work, writing, investing and starting new businesses.

On Power

The world will put you in power; use that power to serve the world not to humiliate the world. We all need each other, therefore treat all with dignity. The best way to exercise power is to be humble.

On Solitude

Loneliness expresses the pain of being alone and solitude expresses the glory of being alone ~ Paul Tillich

The monotony of a quiet life stimulates the creative mind ~ Albert Einstein.

Solitude is very different from a 'time-out' from our busy lives. Solitude is the very ground from which community grows. Whenever we pray alone, study, read, write, or simply spend quiet time away from the places where we interact with each other directly, we are potentially opened for a deeper intimacy with each other ~ Henry Nouwen.

From solitude comes all victory. Think of Jesus in the wilderness, when he was tempted, going for forty days without food. He was all alone. An athletic champion must spend his time alone, training, pushing himself beyond his limits; you cannot do that with friends. An entrepreneur bootstrap to build an empire, they first have to do it alone. There is something special in loneliness but it can only be special if you use your solitude moments wisely.

This is different from the solitude you get when you are bored and sick of everything, when petting your cat in the basement is the best you can do. I am talking about solitude that you get when the world runs away from you, the solitude you get when all options are gone, that moment when your back is against the wall and you are staring right in the face of a monster called life, ready to shred you apart.

That moment when thousands of voices in your head are telling you to throw in the towel, when your body and joints are weak, when your spirit loses focus and all you can do is to let go, when all hope is gone. You are pushed to the limit. That is when a victor fights. That kind of solitude can only be fought by victory mindset. That moment when victory is just but a word without meaning, that is when you need to work hard. These are the moments that define leaders, the moments used by victors to conquer. Keep plugging in, for victory is closer than you can imagine. Just push a little harder and never let all your efforts go in vain.

A mission started is a mission worth accomplishing therefore when you are starting any business, start something of value. Start something that matters. A craving for happiness will be your driving force. In the back of your mind, whisper to yourself that you are a winner. Winners never lose hope.

Everyone has his or her inner shooting stars that they should let shine to cover the whole universe in light. You are a star, never fail to shine.

On Luck

Shallow men believe in luck. Strong men believe in cause and effect ~ Ralph Waldo Emerson

Luck? I don't know anything about luck. I've never banked on it and I am afraid of people who do. Luck to me is something else: Hard work and realizing what opportunity is and what isn't ~ Lucile Ball

Luck is not something you can mention in front of self-made men ~ E. B. White.

Luck is the most futile word to ever appear in the dictionary. It is an ambiguous word without a direction. It is like a stone lying flat ready to be rolled to be in motion. It carries no avalanche that can sweep a mountain down. Luck never exists.

Luck is an illusion created by time wasters; people who pretend to be optimistic yet understand nothing of the foundations of success. If possible, never use the word luck. I do not have a substitute word for it. Why should I substitute something that does not exist?

Even though the word sounds polite and shows that someone cares, it holds no value. All that is, must have a cause. Luck does not agree with this. It assumes that greatness can be achieved effortlessly. Success never just comes. People invest, people work hard, people plan, people engage and exchange and through that great endeavours are being made.

Merriam Dictionary defines luck as the accidental way things happen without being planned. How possible that is, I am not sure.

There are better things that have resulted in success and greatness. Hard work, faith,and resilience are among the attributes of success. What people mean when they talk about luck is chance. Statistically, the probability of one succeeding without working hard is very minimal. Therefore, people should be honest with each other and say, chances are that you are going to pass or fail depending on how prepared you are for the task ahead of you.

This does not mean that we have to be egotistic when we communicate and that is probably why people prefer to use the phrase good luck. It means nothing but sounds polite.
Luck has made people lapse on their journey to success. It has promoted mediocrity and gray scales in achievements. It makes people create a probabilistic room of success without putting in the work. That is why the majority of Americans still believe in winning a lottery they never play.

Statistics never lie, unless they are doctored. To say that it is probable for someone to win the lottery means that person is constantly playing, enrolling and is highly involved in the game. They make it their interest, have faith, hope and invest in it. That is hard work put together with chance not luck.

Something else they forget is that they can compound the entire amount they waste on lottery over a given period of time to get the same amount they would have won in a lottery. Luck does not play well with happiness and mega success.

On A Priori Information on Success

The starting point of all achievements is desire ~ Napoleon Hill.

Success is not a result of spontaneous combustion, you must set yourself on fire ~ Arnold H. Glasow.

Much effort, much prosperity ~ Euripides

Prima facie, success always looks like an overnight tale. It looks like a person woke up one day and found himself living his dream. What we forget to understand is the apriori meaning of success and how it comes about.

Most of the platonic philosophers, including Augustine from Africa, were great thinkers and believers of foreknowledge mainly in form of soul before we reincarnate into humanity. They believed that everything we learn today, we are just reminding ourselves of what we had already known and all of this are stored in a special part of our brain.

They gave examples with how we store information in our brains and we can retrieve it at any time, and get the same feelings, ideas, knowledge and emotions. This can be dangerous because it is the trap that most leaders get into. Take for example; you heard a funny story from a comedian; even if the comedian is not with you, you can still experience through emotions, the joys and pleasures you had when you heard him make a joke. You might find yourself laughing hysterically just as you did when the clown was on stage.

So our brain has that special ability to be comfortable despite the challenges we are going through. This is when people start believing in luck and forget about the work. Leaders always see success before it is achieved and that is what makes them leaders not followers. Now there are two types of leaders.

The Comfortable Leaders

These are the leaders who generate excellent ideas, plan their moves, enter an action with boldness and get too comfortable before they achieve their goals. They visualize success and get that inner contentment of achievements before they are practically changed into reality. Pride becomes their guillotine and arrogance their nose. They are swallowed by their position and their title matters a lot to them.

The fact that you are a founder, CEO, or Executive Director does not mean you are successful. Success involves wisely using those titles to build a sustainable growth of the organization. If you become too contented with success before it arrives, you are a failure.

Sadly, this is the cloud that covers most leaders' vision. The leaders become myopic and lose their sight for success. Success is not about how you start, it is about how you end. Just like marathon runners celebrate after they have won. To lead at the beginning does not mean you are a winner. The comfortable leader gets too comfortable before they are successful.

The Unsettled Leader

Most of the time, the unsettled leader is the one who walks out a winner. They know that time is the scarcest resource we have and they try to maximize its util. They are never betrayed by the titles. The unsettled leader dreams big even after achieving their goals but above all, they understand that celebrations are meant after an achievement, not before.

Leadership is not a position to sit pretty. It is ugly, challenging, and full of attacks. Leadership is an ogre monster that wants to consume you alive. It is a zombie ready to suck your blood and leave you empty. If you cannot run with it, then run away from it. Unsettled leaders understand this concept. They are never confused or betrayed by the prima facia success. They understand that mega success comes after putting in hard work.

Unsettled leaders will do anything within their limits to attain success. They are resilient, never ready to give up easily. They understand that teamwork is good but every member of the team must do his part to yield a synergy.

Leadership needs thick skin. Most people get discouraged when people tell them NO! As a leader and an entrepreneur, when I want to test a person's enthusiasm for his product, I always say no earlier. This kills people's morale. It makes them lose their confidence and shakes the ground beneath their feet. If you can go past my 'No', when pitching your ideas to me then I will understand how strongly you believe in your products.

Leaders understand that not everybody will like their ideas. They expect debates and opposition. They know that it is through opposition and tough competition that they are crowned winners. How can you know that you are a winner if you are competing with yourself? Bring others in the game to truly understand how great you are.

On Orchestrating Leadership

There are two golden rules for an orchestra: start together and finish together. The public doesn't give a damn what goes in between ~ Thomas Beecham.

A man who wants to lead the orchestra must turn his back on the crowd ~ Max Lucado.

Acting is just playing the violin in an orchestra. Directing is being the conductor ~ Jason Bateman.

Never turn your back to the people you are leading, you must face them at all times. Turn your back to the crowd, show them how you conduct well and let them cheer you as you do miracles.

Leadership is like a music concert, a choir that has rehearsed over the years and is ready to perform. However good they might be, they still need a conductor. Surprisingly, the conductor needs them too to make the whole chemistry work. One thing that a good music conductor understands is that the people cheering and jeering become less important in the process of presentation.

It is upon the singers to face the audience. A conductor might just introduce the song when facing the audience and then turn back his face again to face the singers. The wisdom hidden in this analogy leads to:

Focus

A leader needs to focus more on his time by giving right directions. A leader is like a conductor whom everybody depends on including the audience but focuses on a few to impress the multitude. When you put a focus on your team, you learn about them and they also learn your language and communication styles.

Communication

A choirmaster communicates with every part of his body. Gestures, facial expression, hand motions, legs etcetera. Therefore as a leader, you cannot stand behind the choir and expect to get an encore. Clear communication is paramount and your team must be ready and able to read your sign language. Be open and show when you are impressed or not.

Respond to Encore

When the crowd asks for more, give them more. Never overdo it. Show them that they matter; after all, it is them you are performing for. Make them happy. A good leader should know how to balance and add value to their team as well as their audiences. If possible use charms to impress.

Appreciate All

All orchestra leaders understand that the crowd is their biggest customers. After every performance, they always bow down to the crowd and the crowd always shows a standing ovation. Show respect.

On Infinity

Concern yourself more with accepting responsibility than with assigning blame. Let the possibilities inspire you more than the obstacles discourage you ~ Ralph Marston.

You and I are essentially infinite choice-makers. In every moment of our existence, we are in that field of possibilities where we have access to infinity of choices ~ Deepak Chopra

Probable impossibilities are to be preferred to improbable possibilities ~ Aristotle.

There is an infinite amount of wealth to be gained in this world, just as there is an infinite amount of success one can get. Of all the words a true leader should be obsessed with, it's infinity.

It is also wise to understand that to get to infinity, it requires an infinite amount of work. To win infinite success requires infinite resilience and to gain infinite wealth requires infinite planning.

It is also wise to mention that the fact that you are going for infinite wealth does not mean that you can comfortably be greedy. To be self-centered displays your lack of ethics, so never even think of being successful with a greedy mindset.

The fact that you are going for infinite wealth does not mean that you stop being good. "For what will it profit a man if he gains the whole world and forfeits his soul? Or what shall a man give in return for his soul?" (Matthew 16:26). We have to be careful about how we use the infinite power and wealth that we get. Now to get on the road to infinite success one ought to:

Have Succinct Mind

To be a winner, you must have the mindset of a winner and to get to infinite success one must have the infinite mindset. You should remember that dreams are just but illusions of the mind. They are beautiful pictures painted in our thoughts and hung on the wall called memory. We can always see them from a distance but we can never reach them. We can admire the beauty and grandeur they possess but those are only food for our minds. They satisfy our inner feelings and psychological accomplishments yet they do not have any meaning.

Be a Worker Bee

There are so many types of bees; the queen, the special males whose work is mating with the queen before they die, there are the guards who protect the hive but of all these, my favorite is the worker bee.

Worker bees believe that everything is possible. They understand that teamwork is important but synergy can only be reached when each member of the team does his part. They can go miles and miles to look for water, travel for distance to collect nectars and also offer security when needed. They understand that nothing can be achieved without hard work. They believe that they can make infinite honey and that is what they think and do every day.

Even though they work extremely hard, they also have to ensure quality of the final product is good. Of all manufacturers on earth, bees have the greatest quality control department and that can be found on the taste of the honey we get. They never recall their products. They are made once and for all and it is guaranteed to meet the standards.

Get Some Rest

To take a break does not mean you have lost focus. It means that you are ready to re-energize and get back at it. All work and no play made Jack a dull boy. Work hard, play hard and win big. Understand the infinity rule and play it safe. Rest but never get too comfortable while resting. You might lose the vision of infinity.

On the Angel You Don't Know

Learn from yesterday, live for today, hope for tomorrow. The important thing is not to stop questioning ~ Albert Einstein.

Hope is being able to see that there is light despite all of the darkness ~ Desmond Tutu.

Hope is a waking dream ~ Aristotle.

Better the devil you know than the angel you don't know is a phrase that does not work in business. In leadership, it is; better the angel you don't know than the devil you know.
Leadership is full of fights, survival of the fittest, completion, good and bad deals, people who want to finish you, those who want to pounce on you with their claws. They are coming for you. But how can we stay positive without one day hoping to meet an angel we do not know?

Leadership is not a place to sit pretty, it is messy and one must be a thinker and a problem solver. You will be meeting devils every day.

The devil convincing you to hit the snooze button every day when you wake up, yet you know very well that "you snooze, you lose." The devil of war that constantly requires the angel of mediation in the office, the devil of conflict between work and family, the devil of unnecessary temptations and discouragement are all part of leadership. If you don't have hopes in an angel you do not know, you are going to lose the game. To meet this angel, one ought to:

Be a Constant Seeker

Your pursuit of success should be stronger than your will to give up. Knowing that nothing comes easy, the amount of success you are going to get is directly proportional to the effort you apply.

Have Hope

To overcome the devil, one ought to know that there is a reward to every good fight fought. It requires belief and a constant reminder that you can achieve it all if you give it your all. To believe in an angel you do not know, shows a strong commitment in your vision, mission and value statements. Those who are hopeful go through a lot of difficulties but they are never discouraged by the predicaments they meet on their route to success. Have hope that the angel you do not know will bring good fortune according to the work you have done. Why put effort in ideas you do not believe in?

Never Underestimate Your Efforts

A lot of successful people started from the bottom up. They knew that they were weaker than the challenges they were meeting but they understood the power of resilience.

Be Ready to Give

There is power in giving. The more we give the more we get. Giving does not only mean financial provision to those in needs or to a charity or to a church. It means offering all you can to people who need it the most.

My pastor, who is also my mentor, once talked to me about what giving back to God means. It is not about just giving tithes; we can give our time, resources, harvest, family services and to glorify God. For whatever good we do today, we are doing it for the divine being with a greater good and that is God.

Be an Avid Reader

Learning is very important. The only way to stop making the same mistakes over and over again is to learn at least one thing every day. If you do not have time to sit in class, buy a book and read it on your way to and from work. Most commuters take roughly forty-five minutes on their way to work. In a day they spend ninety minutes doing nothing. If you can use those ninety minutes to learn something you did not know yesterday, you are getting closer to meeting that angel.

Dream and Act

I have talked to so many people who tell me that they want to start their own businesses, how much they hate their workplace and how they want to be free by starting something of their own where they are their own bosses.

Well and good but if you are starting something new because you want freedom then sorry but you are going to fail! If you cannot handle working from 9:00 am till 5:00 pm, you think you can start a business that constantly needs your attention?

I am not sure where you are in your journey to success. Maybe you are reading this book and you fall under the category of freedom dreamers. If you want to be free, resign from your work and enjoy your time. Leading a business of any kind is so stressful.

Staying Calm

Perseverance is the hard work you do after getting tired of the hard work you already did ~ Newt Gingrich.

Calm mind brings inner strength and confidence, so that is important for good health ~ Dalai Lama.

When adversity strikes, that is when you have to be the most calm. Take a step back, stay strong, stay grounded and press on ~LL Cool J.

Business and leadership are where the unexpected frequently occur. Some news can destroy you and even result in serious medical problems if not well taken care of. There is only one solution to entrepreneurship and leadership bad news; stay calm.

It is not easy to stay calm when bad news is fresh. When you are disappointed, discouraged and covered in rubble. That moment when your roof caves in and walls crumble apart, when all hope is gone and failure is what you are left with. The worst is yet to come and that is why you need to be calm. Here are some important fruits of staying calm.

Decision Making

When your world is shattered, it is highly probable that the decisions you are going to make are going to cost you more. It is hard to make informed decision when you are torn apart. It is therefore better to recollect yourself before making decisions especially when you are angry or highly disappointed.

Take your Time

If any moment when patience become a virtue is when things go wrong. It is hard to stay patient and calm in such a time. Therefore, best solutions are not made when people are mad. Take your time to calm down and see the challenge as a mere hurdle that tests your genuine heroic strengths behind your efforts.

Build Trust

Nobody trusts a leader who paces up and down in the time of turmoil. People tend to love those leaders who are brave or can put on smile despite the biggest challenge an organization might be going through. Once people learn of your confidence and ability to take a beating, they will look at you as their hero. A person they can confidently confide in to change their lives.

Positive Thought Process

It is often very easy to switch into retaliation mode by making hasty decisions when angry. Staying calm will make you sober and start thinking positively instead of negatively. Staying calm will make you act on your failures and challenges. Making decisions when you are angry and frustrated is a sign that you are reacting to the challenge making the challenge bigger than what it actually is. You should be controlling the challenge not the challenge controlling you. This is a concept that is widely adopted by those who go for mega success.

Despite the fact that you are challenged, never react but rather act on solving the problem. Challenges are there to be solved not to be fueled. By making decisions on the spot when you are not emotionally stable, you show a weakness that can be read by many.

Take Deep Breaths

It might sound silly prima facie but try it when you are rattled. It really does help. Different people have different ways of calming themselves down. Some people find solace in crying while I personally find solace in retrieving and thinking critically about the next step. I try not to work in panic mode. If the stress is more than I can handle then I just take a nap and wake up when I am fresh. Take a few deep breaths and make a decision on the best and realistic solution for the challenge. I then immediately start working on it and the more I get done the more my stress and anger diminishes.

Find your philosophy of dealing with such challenges and be disciplined at implementing it.

Never Communicate

Anytime our organization faces a challenge, I try to cut all communications from emails, phone calls, social media, texts and anything that can show my emotions at that moment. People can read your emotions in the way you communicate with them even if it is not a face to face communication. Let nobody read your emotions when you are rattled. People will always think of you as a calm leader who knows and understands how to solve problems.

In some organizations, you might need to call a crisis meeting. Make sure that before you sit down with your team to inform them of the challenge, that you have digested the problem and have come up with possible ways to reduce the magnitude of the challenge so that your team can see it as a minor thing that they can act on and solve. Any moment you magnify a challenge, your team will magnify it and make the challenge look twice as big as it is.

Mega success achievers understand these factors making them great problem solvers with high emotional control. For mega success, remember to stay calm.

On Velocity of Success

The speed of the boss is the speed of the team ~ Lee Iacocca.

Fix your eyes on perfection and you make almost everything speed towards it ~ William Ellery Channing.

If your history does not shock you, then you probably have not transformed. Success waits for no man. It is always on the run. It runs faster than the fastest man alive. It is a thunderbolt that hits and destroys in the twinkle of an eye. If success was a thunderbolt, you have to be lightning arresters to capture it or else it will destroy you.

Big dreamers are slumbers; they waste their time visualizing greatness instead of focusing on how to become pragmatists. Sadly, a majority of people fall into this category including a lot of entrepreneurs. Even though they know procrastination results in failure, they fail to take action to do what ought to be done.

Since success is constantly in motion, one must move faster than it to catch up with it. It never favors cowards or those who fear competition. Success gives in to the brave, those who can be bold enough to face it's scary looks.

The reason why champions practice harder is not because they want to beat their rivals but because they want to catch up with the greatness of success. The more you win the tougher the race gets. Learn how to build team synergy and let every member of the team do their work diligently. This can only happen when you have clear communication with your team.

Success is not a sprint. It is a marathon where leading is not important but winning is. An athlete can lead the race until the last second when his or her rival beats him or her to the finish line. When you are leading, keep your pace and time yourself.

We cannot talk of velocity of success without talking about time. Velocity is a vector quantity that must have a specific direction. Without direction it's termed as speed. Therefore to win, you must calculate how far you are from success and how long it is going to take you to get there. Time is of the essence. It is the most underutilized and abused resource I once lived with roommates who wanted me to have at least 3 nights a week doing nothing with them and just talking and making jokes. At that time, I had already started our international charity organization and an online book promotion platform by the name of Spill Books. Since I was just starting all these, I had a part-time job to take care of my living expenses as I was also planning to go to school. I knew that this was not good for my health but I had to prioritize my activities with every twenty-four hours I had in a day. I never forget that success comes from solitude and those were my solitude moments.

What makes success a tough race is that the faster you run the faster it goes and the more people are pulling you back. They are there to grab your shirt and waste your energy. Instead of running to succeed, you might find yourself running and pulling others who do not want you to prosper. You have less energy to waste. Get rid of those who want to hold you back. Time is a factor and to beat success you first have to beat the race.

On Staying True

I have always tried to stay true to my authentic self ~ Katie Couric.

Make it clear upfront what the aim of the company is. Stay true to your authentic vision ~ Peter Diamandis

God blessed us with what is termed as free will. We can wisely use it or foolishly abuse it. The decision is all ours. But how do you use this type of freedom? Do you choose to do good because of the repercussions that the government has set to curb the vilest offenders? Or do you do good because it is good to do good? Now the latter idea might sound like circular reasoning. You have the freedom and will to discredit it. That is how big the choices we make are.

Of the most important decisions we can make on will as fallible beings are to either remain true to people or not. The worst we can do to ourselves is to lie to ourselves. Remaining true to yourself is a bold step towards success. It means putting yourself in the limelight and accepting your strengths and weaknesses.

We can pretend to be who we are not. We can act like celebrities that the media has poisoned our minds with, but what remains is that we are wasting our time living other people's lives. Any moment you are living somebody else's life, you become a prisoner to your idol. This is a self-imposed slavery that you can easily get out of. All it takes is to know how we use the gift that God has given us. The gift of freedom of choice.

It is not surprising to know that human beings are the only creatures that have refused to accept to be who they are. All this is because of free will. For success, you have to do things you do not want to do, plan things you do not want to plan and read books you do not want to read.

Mega success is only achieved at greater risk, if you haven't taken risks, you haven't lived. Entrepreneurship needs action, act in faith and hope will take you there. In every effort you put towards achieving a goal without backing up, there is always a reward for it.

In all the choices you are making, consider giving your best in everything you do. Since the discouraging voice is always louder than the encouraging voice, it is better to choose the low voice. It is the voice that gently pushes you to do things beyond your limit. It will be the quiet console when the pain is too much. It is the gentle voice advising you that you can do it if you take another step. It never fails, but we choose to fail our inner choice to success.

Just as all leaders are thinkers and all thinkers are artists, one ought to craft his or her leadership style. That is a choice. Use free will to propel yourself to higher ground. We are all made the same and if one person can do it, you can do it better than they.

When it comes to freedom of choice and will, there are only two things: you are either willing to do something or not. The choice you make now is going to define your future and who you are going to be tomorrow. Use free will to make wise choices. And above all, learn how to be true to yourself. It is a must-have philosophy to succeed.

On Possibility and Failure

My favorite words are possibilities, opportunities and curiosity. I think if you are curious, you create opportunities and then if you open the doors, you create possibilities ~ Mario Testino.

We all have possibilities we don't know about. We can dream things we don't even dream we can do ~ Dale Carnegie.

A lot of people fail not because they are incapable of doing something productive but because they choose to define themselves with failure. To succeed in life, one ought to have a success mindset. Define yourself with success and it will come true.

Failure

Over seventy-five percent of business startups fail within ten years, meaning that at some point, one must fail in one area of life. To fail does not mean you are incapable; it simply means that you are doing the right thing the wrong way.

It is also important to know that there is no surgical accuracy in success. Every business has the potential to succeed and to fail. What you need to know is how not to repeat the same mistakes over and over. There are people who started from zero to hero. The forty-fourth president of the United States of America, Barack Obama became the president without having turns of wealth. He is the second president after Nixon to get into power without riches. What they mastered was how to avoid repeating their old mistakes. There are areas they failed at but they were never held back by challenges. They were propelled to power by their charisma, boldness, and clarity of their message.

It is always said that people are reluctant to change but that is not true. People are always in dire need of change only that they do not trust the leaders coming in with change. You do not need a proven record of leadership to lead, what you need is to assure people that you can impact their lives.

I look at how much people look at the past experience in résumé before they hire a potential candidate and it breaks my heart. The worst was when a company that I worked for had me as part of the hiring team and the candidates shortlisted for interviews were judged by their last names. This is not in a developing nation but in North America.

In such cases, you do not expect growth. There can be an upward growth trend but I can assure you that it is short lived.

Possibility

All leaders are thinkers and all thinkers are artists, therefore craft your leadership style. We all can attain greatness and succeed if we push ourselves to the limit. Possibility is a strong term that everybody should believe in. If your actions result in value in other people's lives, then you are going to succeed.

The power of possibility gives us hope that we can not only see the light at the end of the tunnel, but that we are also determined to reach it. Sometimes we can see the light at the end of the tunnel and think that we are already there. If you still do not have light on your hand, keep going. Our state of mind is naturally wired to go on a comfort zone however terrible the conditions we are in. This can be deceiving especially when we are getting closer to success.

So if you have a vision that you hold dear to your heart, write an inspiring phrase and put it in a frame and hang it on every wall where you are. The phrase should be "it is possible!"
Leaders are those who are brave enough to act on their challenges with a hope of defeating them. Believe that it is possible and you are half way there.

On Confidence and Boldness

Believe in yourself. Have faith in your abilities. Without a humble but reasonable confidence in your own powers you cannot be successful or happy ~ Norman Vincent Peale

If you have no confidence in self, you are twice defeated in the race of life ~ Marcus Garvey.

When you are going to start a project, make sure it is of great value. Why would you start a business that does not add value to anybody's life? That is where confidence starts. Lack thereof means lack of value. If you understand that you are valueless, then you have all the freedom to lack confidence.

Why Confidence?

Human beings are doubting beings. Any moment you present an idea, people will try to refute it, shutter it, shred it and dump it in garbage. Nobody will trust you. The only way to gain other people's trust is confidence, enthusiasm, and charisma. How well do you communicate your ideas? How passionate are you about your product? Do you believe in your product? Does your body language exhibit your confidence and trust in your business?

All these might be too much to handle in the first five minutes if not less when you are communicating a new idea. That is why confidence is important and confidence goes hand in hand with value.

Value

Chema chajiuza, kibaya cha jitembeza is a Swahili pun, a common language in East Africa meaning, whatever is good markets itself and whatever is bad does not. It is easier to sell an idea that adds value to people's lives than an idea that does not.

Think of Google and how it has changed the Internet world. Google has actually become a verb in our world today. That is how you know that your business is adding value to people's lives.

You do not have to be at Google's level to impact the world and gain confidence. If you are truly adding value in the market today, it is guaranteed you will sell. Another way to gain this confidence is by telling a story. People relate well to real time, real life stories. If you dug a borehole that is providing clean and safe drinking water to 30,000 people in a developing world somewhere, that is a powerful story.

Confidence is in and of itself a platform for success. You only need to master the skills required to communicate with your audience.

Preparedness

One ought to master this trait to be successful. I once attended a meeting of a pastor who demolished all my foundations which left me defenseless yet I had all the good stories of what our organization had done in developing economies. Prepare ahead of time; get to know your audience before you share your story with them. Have a connecting point.

If you think time is too short to research about them, use the power of Internet to know about whom you are sharing your ideas with and then communicate in a language that they can understand. Talk of things you share in common and build rapport. Knowing your audience will give you enough confidence to prepare for any questions and/or what to share with them.

Have a Blue Print

It is until you are in a real need of success that you will succeed. To truly succeed, you need a blueprint. This is your guidance, map and your route to success. It should be a constant reminder of the change that people need. Lead with confidence, stay true to your people.

On Being Michelangelo

There is a real magic in enthusiasm. It spells the difference between mediocrity and accomplishments ~ Norman Vincente Peale

It is wretched taste to be gratified with mediocrity when the excellent lies before us ~ Isaac D'Israeli.

Michelangelo was a sculptor, painter, architect, poet and engineer of Renaissance. His works inspired and had greatly influenced the Western arts. All of his works have made him the most celebrated artist ever since 16th century. A leader should learn a few if not all of Michelangelo's traits.

Be a Multitasking Guru

Michelangelo never relied on one thing for a living. He did it all and that is why he lives to be the most celebrated and influential artist to ever roam the face of the earth. He was a
sculptor, painter, architect, poet and engineer. He never stopped at one thing. To be a great leader, one ought to learn to do it all. You do not have to be exactly who Michelangelo was but you should understand a number of fields for networking purposes.

People like to network with informed people. In the world today, technology has made it very easy for us to gather information and learn about the world. Make good use of it.

Be Determined

In everything Michelangelo did, he did it very well. His carvings and drawings are still admired all over the world. In whatever you are doing, be determined to give the best. The world only crowns those who are great at what they do. With the competition today, people will only buy the best, listen to the best and support the best. You can be on top of all these if you are determined enough to be the greatest.

Never Create Room for Mediocrity

Michelangelo did his best in whatever he was doing. He perfected his skills and became the master giving masterpieces. The world is full of mediocre people, and although less room left for it, many people still find themselves in mediocrity. If Michelangelo could not have done his best, I could not have found anything to talk about. It is highly probable that there were so many artists who never perfected their skills and never astound people by their brush work. You have all the free will to choose who you want to be. Be Michelangelo not any other artists who died unsung.

Resilience

It took Michelangelo four years to paint the Sistine ceiling. He did all of this work lying upside down and it is said that that is how he developed a problem with his spine. Real leaders never believe in impossibilities. Everything is possible and they know that there is gain after every pain. Let your dark moments in life inspire hope in you that a morning is coming. There is always a reward in every struggle you successfully go through. Mega success is the final picture of struggle and hard work; therefore, never give up. If Michelangelo had given up painting the world's greatest ceiling ever, we would have had nothing to praise him for. Do your best today. You might not be celebrated or congratulated but a generation is coming after you that will write and sing about you.

Be Unique

Paint the pictures that have never been painted before, do the work that has never been done before, write on topics that have never been written on before, visualize the things that have never been imagined before and plan the things that have never been planned before. The Sistine ceiling would not have been famous if there were thousands or even hundreds of the same. Create some original ideas and make them a reality.

Inspire Competitors

To be crowned a winner, you must have contenders; better off if your competitors crown you one. To win you have to beat someone and therefore embrace competition. They will advance your thinking and anyway, why think small if you have the freedom to think big? Take risks. Sometimes the greater the risk, the greater; the reward therefore, try. If you lose, that is not the end of the world, laugh at your mistakes and never repeat them. But before you risk, do your homework. You want to have as minimal liability as possible, better off if you can have none.

On Getting Inspired by Inspiring

Good actions give strengths to ourselves and inspire good actions in others ~ Plato

Creative thinking inspires ideas. Ideas inspire change ~ Barbara Januszkiewicz

Inspirational leaders need to have a winning mentality in order to inspire respect. It is hard to trust in the leadership of someone who is half-hearted about their purpose, or only sporadic in focus or enthusiasm ~ Sebastian Coe

Nothing inspires an individual like seeing people he or she inspired succeeding. Those who inspire others to greatness are either themselves great or on their way to greatness. I have not seen a successful person who is not willing to stretch a helping hand to support those who thirst and crave for success. It is also important to note that for one to succeed, you must create unlimited gates for others to succeed. Get inspired by inspiring.

Even though everybody qualifies to inspire others to achieve their dreams, some do it better than others. Those who are great at inspiring others often have traits like:

Hard Working

Those who understand that the only shortcut to success is through hard work are always great at inspiring others to act. Since they themselves are a living testimony of success, they can lead by example through sharing their stories and showing others the right way to greatness. Greatness just never comes, it takes work and relentlessness. That is why you need to master this philosophy.

Relentless

It is important to differentiate relentlessness with stubbornness. While stubbornness has got bits of arrogance in it, relentlessness is the act of staying positive despite all the negatives that one might be going through. Those who are relentless believe not only in themselves but they understand that anybody can achieve their dreams only if they persist.

Big Dreamers

To inspire others, you must have a full force driving you to do things beyond your efforts. How can you motivate others to be successful if you are a failure? A blind man can never show the way to other blind men. Those enroot to success or those who are already there are the ones who can better inspire others to greatness.

Invest in Themselves

Those who inspire others to greater actions are themselves open to learning bigger things. They are avid readers and appreciate education. One of the best things you can do to yourself is to feed your brain with positive ideas. You can never give what you do not have, therefore to inspire others to act; you must first have been inspired and acted. Books are written to be read not to fill our shelves. I would rather walk in an office and find the occupant's desk covered in books than walk in an office where books are tidy on the shelves but he or she does not know the contents of the books he or she is keeping. If you have a book that you have not read and you think it can build you on your journey to success, read it.

Wise Time Users

How many hours do you spend on the internet doing nothing? How many hours do you spend watching movies and TV shows? How many hours do you spend sleeping? How many hours do you spend talking nonsense with people who do not impact your life to greatness? How many hours do you spend in procrastination? Well enough, you might say that you do not have any of these negative time wasting habits, okay, how did you spend your last three hours? Did you do anything positive? Did you touch a life? Did you add value to someone's life? What role did you play to make the world a better place for humanity?

They Go Past Their Limits

Limits are not there to bar you from success but to make you a champion, a warrior and a hero. To be crowned a hero, one must first go through all the hurdles and barriers on the way.
Success just never comes. It must be earned through hard work. Hurdles exist to prune the lazy and to promulgate hard workers as successful. Those who are great at inspiring others know and understand that barriers are a source of motivation towards realization of one's efforts. Hard work pays. Therefore, to earn you must work hard.

On Respecting the Journey

Sometimes it's the journey that teaches you a lot about your destination ~ Drake.

By prevailing over all obstacles and distractions, one may unfailingly arrive at his chosen goal or destination ~ Christopher Columbus.

One of the best paradoxes of leadership is a leader's need to be both stubborn and open-minded. A leader must insist on sticking to the vision and stay on course to the destination. But he must be open-minded during the process ~ Simon Sinek.

Life is a journey; it has twists and turns. Sometimes it takes you through the plains, sometimes through the mountaintops and sometimes on fields and plains where the horizons are clear.

What you do today is what defines your future. If you put in hard work today, then the probability is high that you are going to be prosperous in the future. If you chose to live carelessly, life will give you less. There is abundance in store for those who never give up. The mighty are crowned and the lazy are taken out of the equation.

Like Darwin's theory of adaptive evolution, which states that there is a presence of heritable genetic variation that results in fitness difference. Life has got a natural way of selecting the chosen few who can make it to the top. A lot of people are mediocre because they are either too comfortable with mediocrity or because of fear. They either fear failure or fear success. Either way they do not have the guts to try.

If we define success in terms of mediocrity then we are limiting ourselves and restricting our freedom to venture and adventure. There is unlimited success out there to be won. And after victory, there is even more work to challenge your own victory. Any animal when pushed to the maximum can do unimaginable work.

When making decisions, try coming up with ideas that do not allow life's adaptive selection theory to prune you out. Dream big and act big, and after succeeding, do it even bigger!

Those who respect their journey today understand that their future heavily relies on their actions. They do all they can to build a rapport with everybody, especially those who can elevate their potentials to higher grounds. Leaders and entrepreneurs do this most of the time. As an entrepreneur, I have learned that building a stable network today is one way of constructing a platform for our organizations future. We are defined by the potentials we put in today.

When you succeed, remember those people who built you, those who never gave up on you and saw the inner power within you and trusted you enough to invest in you. They are still part of your life; therefore, draw them even closer. Most of these people will already be successful and/or on their way to success. Hard work pays. Do what you can and let God do the rest. Our work should not spare us from God but draw us even closer to him. God brought us into this world to be stewards of his blessings in our lives. We own nothing therefore we should give back to God what belongs to him. How beautiful can it be when all leaders and entrepreneurs can say, "Lord here I am, take me, all of me and use me for your glory." Give thanks.

On Self Contained Rivalry

Never create rivals other than rivalry within yourself. It is always tempting to see other contestants as a threat, but it may surprise you to say they are not. Your closest competitor is within you, you dine, walk, wake up and go to bed every day with him or her. When choosing your rivals, first chose yourself.

So why do we need to build self-contained rivalry?

Improvement

With self-contained rivalry, you only compare yourself with yourself. Self-contained rivalry is when you decide to compete with who you were yesterday with the aim of being a better person today. If you slept in yesterday, you need to try and beat that today and wake up at 6 o'clock. If you procrastinated and wasted five hours of your day, you need to adjust that today and use your time wisely. This self-comparison will motivate you to do greater things without knowing.

Strength Differentials

Your strengths are not my strengths. We are all different. If I want to be who I am not, then I am only punishing myself. If someone else is better than me on something, I should be there to motivate him and encourage him to do more but remember to keep the praise genuine. Do what you do best and better off if you do more than you can imagine. Go beyond your limits, plan big and act bigger.

Weakness Differentials

My weaknesses are not what your weaknesses are. We cannot all be the same. There is a common mistake that couples make when dating, they all look at the similarities and congruence yet they forget to look at how they differ. An example is what type of movies does she like to watch? What type of music does he listen to? What type of restaurants does she go to? While all these are important, it is also good to focus on your personal differences. What makes you weak and how can you both complement each other? That is what is important. Never pick battles unless you are certain that you can win them. It is better if you can work on your weaknesses and make them your greatest strengths. Should you not be able to do this perfectly and then hire those who can do it to complement you?

Any moment you make a decision to be better than whom you were yesterday; you are on the track to win big games. Self-contained rivalry is a philosophy of greatness. It leads to higher results. Know that your greatest rival is who you were yesterday. Start every day with new ideas, but with a goal of doing more and being better than you were previous day.

On Stress

Being in control of your life and having realistic expectations about your day-to-day challenges are the keys to stress management, which is perhaps the most important ingredient to living a happy, healthy and rewarding life ~ Marilu Henner.

There's going to be stress in life, but it's your choice whether to let it affect you or not ~ Velerie Bertinelli.

A lot of people stress for no apparent reason leading them to lose hope and burn out of great ideas that could have revolutionized the world. You never know, people might be waiting for the idea you are giving up on. If Elon Musk failed to get a fourth trial on his Space-X project, how could we know that private entities could fly in space and come back? What if Einstein gave up on the light bulb experiment? The reason why we fail is because we build a negative attitude towards a challenge leading us to ask "What if?" That is where we go wrong.

A leader should then build a plan on how to handle stress. Most entrepreneurs are called thick skinned but the reality is that they are also human beings with feelings and get heartbroken. The only thing they are good at is handling stress. They endure discomfort and they develop a unique hope that they can do it and that anything can be achieved if you try harder. Success is not for the faint of heart. It is for those who know how to compartmentalize their stress. So what is compartmentalization of stress?

Even though the psychology definition of this word is an unconscious psychological defense mechanism used to avoid cognitive dissonance, or the mental discomfort and anxiety caused by a person's having conflicting values, cognitions, emotions and beliefs; my definition is to divide or separate stress into distinct parts and sections that you can handle.

This is where people go wrong. They mix stress of all kinds into one large rolling ball of snow leading to accumulation of unnecessary "what ifs" that can wear you out leading to despair. Any moment you bring more than two stresses together, you are desperately hunting for failure. It takes time to compartmentalize stress. The reason being, that human beings have default reactions to different situations. Some things will send you into panic mode and if you have not learned how to handle panic then it can build up to a life threatening defect.

Entrepreneurs and leaders handle a lot of stresses. From family, internal business stress, customer stress, board member stress, and financial stress among others. If you put all these together, you cannot be functional at all. It is therefore important to address every stress differently and at an appropriate time. Matthew 6:25-34:

"Therefore I tell you, do not be anxious about your life, what you will eat or what you will drink, nor about your body, what you

will put on. Is not life more than food, and the body more than clothing? *26Look at the birds of the air: they neither sow nor reap nor gather into barns, and yet your heavenly Father feeds them. Are you not of more value than they? 27And which of you by being anxious can add a single hour to his span of life? 28And why are you anxious about clothing? Consider the lilies of the field, how they grow: they neither toil nor spin, 29yet I tell you, even Solomon in all his glory was not arrayed like one of these. 30But if God so clothes the grass of the field, which today is alive and tomorrow is thrown into the oven, will he not much more clothe you, O you of little faith? 31Therefore do not be anxious, saying, 'What shall we eat?' or 'What shall we drink?' or 'What shall we wear?' 32For the Gentiles seek after all these things, and your heavenly Father knows that you need them all. 33But seek first the kingdom of God and his righteousness, and all these things will be added to you.*

34"Therefore do not be anxious about tomorrow, for tomorrow will be anxious for itself. Sufficient for the day is its own trouble."

What this means is that as much as we would like to worry about the future, it is important not to worry much but rather try and solve the problem that needs to be addressed. It is easy to cave in and bow down to pressure from different walks of life but victory follows those who chase it.

When I was taking my undergraduate, just like most of us do, I took almost two months stressing about my future because I could not afford the costly tuition and as an international student, I could not borrow student loans like others did. The more I stressed, the less I got done and the more work kept piling on my desk leading to more frustrations. At this point, it is easier to quit than to face your fears. Then I realized that I was stressing over nothing, I was not kicked out of school, I did not borrow any loans yet I owe my school nothing. This does not mean that I lived a good life during my university time. I almost ended up in the streets but by the grace of God, I did not.

Stress is one way that a hero gets tested. If you are malleable to stress heat then you probably need to work more on your resilience *"Count it all joy, my brothers when you meet trials of various kinds, for you know that the testing of your faith produces steadfastness. And let steadfastness have its full effect, that you may be perfect and complete, lacking in nothing."*(James 1:2-4).

Great leaders know that they need to stay calm during stressful moments. It shows that you are courageous and bold but if you pace up and down during trying times then people will lose faith in you. People like bold and courageous leaders and the only way to show these attributes is when you or your office is facing a challenge. After the third time of Elon Musk's failure to send the private rocket to space, he said that he never gives up until his mission is all done. What a spirit. He went ahead and bought a whole new warehouse, renovated it and built a space ship in it and on their fourth trial they made it. Great things never come easy and stress can make great dreams become great failures. Divide your stress into family, work, friends or any other department that fits you best and never mix your stresses. Deal with them individually and never waste time thinking more about it than required. Once you have stress, look at it as an opportunity to grow and show the world that you are capable as a leader. Proving that you are a capable leader makes you go an extra mile because you will have people backing you up in all steps when they see how strongly you move despite the challenges.

How to Find Mentors

I am not a teacher, but an awakener ~ Robert Frost

Do not train a child to learn by force or harshness; but direct them to it by what amuses their minds, so that you may be better able to discover with accuracy the peculiar bent of the genius of each ~ Plato.

It can be awkward approaching strangers or people you are not used to talking to and asking them to be your mentor. Even though it is highly advisable to get a mentor, a lot of people do not have them because of lack of guts to ask people to be their counselor. It takes a lot of courage and vulnerability to get a mentor to share your world and life with.

Mentor programs are peer-learning programs and often times result to a symbiotic benefit. It is a give and get back, a two-way street where people who want to see change, development and growth encourage and guide each other. It is important to ask yourself the reasons why you need a mentor. What is it that you lack that you can only get in a mentor? You must also ask yourself; how is your mentor going to benefit from you? How will time spent with you lead to growth for your mentor? To get a mentor one ought to:

Identify Potential Mentors

I personally have three mentors; a self-development mentor or a coach, a business mentor and a spiritual mentor who happens to be my associate pastor. These are people I look after and they act as my role models. I admire their lifestyle, their work ethics and discipline.

When I was looking for a spiritual mentor, I gathered courage and asked my pastor to be my mentor, he prayed about it and told me that he had never mentored anybody and so thought that our time together would not benefit any of us. That was an honest answer even though it was discouraging to me. It is normal to get rejection therefore never give up.

Ask as Many as Possible

This is something I learned the hard way. I had an assumption that my pastor was going to say yes to me when I asked him and that turned out to be false. It killed my enthusiasm and affected my spiritual life too. I was not ready for a "NO!"

It is, therefore, important to have a plan B. People who you think can help you grow in whatever area you want to improve in. Never lose hope, however many people you have to ask before you get a yes. By the time I asked my current spiritual mentor who was not even an associate pastor at the time, I had asked 3 others who told me almost the same thing as my head pastor told me. Never take "No," personal.

Make it Symbiotic

It can be draining to give and get nothing in return. Something I advise those I mentor and coach is always to give more than they get. How can your mentor benefit from meeting you once a week or twice a month? Before you get, be ready to give and after you give, be ready to give more. I can testify that the more you give, the more you get. Never just give, show that you truly and genuinely care for people. Giving can be in form of time, advice, prayers, not only material giving.

Common Interest

There are very successful people in areas that you are interested in. The best way to ask for a mentor which has always worked for me is to identify their strength, a breakthrough or a major success they have achieved and let them know that you admire that effort. Then ask them for at least 30 minutes of their time in a month to meet up and get to hear and learn from their stories. They should clearly know that you are interested in the same field they are in.

While doing this, it is important to know that people like being appreciated, congratulated and praised but remember never to overdo it. People also like to talk about themselves, therefore listen and ask as many questions as possible.

Accept Challenges

This is how I make sure that I score the second meeting with my mentors. Before we end our meeting, I always ask if there are projects they would like me to start researching if I want to see improvement in my life. I always give them a month or two before I give them results. Accept challenges they give you and act towards them because the same challenges are what made them heroes.

Think Organically

We always want to make things happen, show how smart and determined we are but guess what, a lot of successful people are not interested in that. It is important therefore to start thinking organically. Thinking organically is a strategic way of building relationships based on common interests hustle-free. Never make it look like you are trying so hard. Just make it happen.

Let it look as natural as it can get and remember to do your homework.

Respect

You are dealing with busy people and if anybody has allowed you to get an hour of his or her lifetime, you should appreciate it. Bring a notebook and a pen. Avoid typing on your electronic as it kills morale and shows lack of attention.

I also learned from my friend who is the Chief Operations Officer of Canadian Cancer Center that you should always remember to send the meeting minutes to anybody you meet with in less than 24 hours of your meeting. Even if it is a phone call or a Skype meeting, write the main points down and send them via email. This way, you let them know that you are keen on following details and that you are really interested in growth and change you want.

If you do these, you are not only going to be successful but you are going to achieve mega success.

On Major Functions of a Leader

A leader is one who knows the way, goes the way, and shows the way ~ John C Maxwel.

Innovation distinguishes between a leader and a follower ~ Steve Jobs.

A good leader takes a little more than his share of the blame, a little less than his share of the credit ~ Arnold Glasow.

I have mentioned a number of times in my literatures that a leader without philosophy is not a leader. If we look at it logically, something cannot be and be at the same time. We cannot talk about leadership without philosophy otherwise we are contradicting ourselves. Leadership therefore is a philosophy.

Leadership is a means to an end. Every leader works toward ending a challenge and improving life standards on the surface of our earth. Ask yourself this "what do you do every day to warrant this transformation leading to an end?" Are you solving anything every day to make the world a better place? One does not have to do it alone and that is why we need to build cohesive teams. It takes strong leadership skills to get an organization of any kind going. Some of the functions of a leader in an organization are:

To Attract People

Through compelling vision and a purpose for better lives, a leader can build an affinity towards his goal by communicating his dreams well. Based on experience, people will give you attention and the attention either fades away or grows stronger based on what you communicate to them. Do you have a story? How is your story going to impact your audience? Do you leave your audience trapped in a cage where their only option is to respond to your call?

A leader should be there to collect and draw people in from all walks of life to accomplish a goal. Once you have attracted people, a second challenge arises.

Retaining People

This is one of the most difficult things and it heavily relies on your first challenge and that is to collect people. When collecting people, make sure you have a strong reason for bringing them together. To get it right, you need to ask yourself or your team this question, "Why are we bringing people together?" What is your overarching thesis? Or what is your strongest point of bringing people together?

If you can build a strong point, then you have managed to achieve the first step of attracting people hence moving to the second phase and that is retaining people. Remember that you will be dealing with busy people and they are sacrificing their time to work on their businesses, stay with their families or enjoy their hard earned wealth to be with you.

Never make the mistake of inviting people when you are not ready. I once had our major event of the year cancelled almost a week before the event. We had already invited dignitaries and some prominent persons in the business world. As embarrassing as it was, we had to cancel the event quoting unforeseen reasons. Two things I learned from this:

1. People will trust you more when you are honest to cancel such event because they understand that you know that their time is of value and you do not want to waste it.

2. Once people trust you, they will follow you because they know that you care about them. The worst thing to do to a fellow human being is to waste their time. Time only happens once and once it is gone, it can never be brought back.

Grow People

If your idea transforms lives, improves humanity and makes the world a better place to live in, you are a leader. After retaining people, it is now your role to grow people. For this type of growth, a leader must be open with the knowledge he has and freely share it with the people. As you share your ideas, it is important to know that nobody is all-knowing therefore avoid arrogance and embrace learning from others too.

Listen to everybody, but pick your advice from a few. Wisdom shared is wisdom saved. It is a long term investment that pays back when your disciples become heroes. Never hide an idea if you can communicate it. Our life is so fragile, we are here today and tomorrow we are gone. Why leave with all the intelligence and wisdom if you can share it with future generation? Educate people and people will teach you in return.

Nobody wants to be in a place with no growth. That is also why innovations and inventions spring after every hour. You are a priest and your followers are your disciples. Teach them the right way. Educate them to succeed. As a leader, remember to collect, retain and grow people.

You Are a Star so Shine

In order for the light to shine so brightly, the darkness must be present ~ Francis Bacon.

There are no right and wrong ways to work in this business, but there are some basic common-sense practices. Work very, very hard and always be prepared; never give up; and once you get the job, give them more than they ever expected: - Shine! ~ Jimmy Smits.

I once watched a sermon by Louis Giglio on how great God is. I was amazed by how he weaved science and creationism to produce a beautiful picture of how great our God is. Over the years, I have had a strong interest in our terrestrial world, the stars, the universe and what goes on beyond our solar system. Unfortunately I have never had enough information even after keenly following the two satellites that were sent by NASA to the alien's world; Voyager 1 and Voyager 2. It warms my heart to see people like Elon Musk working towards conquering other planets with a big dream of dying on Mars but not on impact. That is very ambitious.

From Giglio's sermon, I saw stars bigger than our brightest star, the sun. Some were scary red, some were royal blue among other constellations I have never imagined in my life.

But one thing he said as a joke was that some of the stars we see at night and sing to them, "twinkle, twinkle little star, how I wonder what you are." His comment was that those stars are so big and so far away and ferocious and that is why we think they are small. They are a wonder, some bigger than the orbit of the earth around the sun. Some of them take a million of light years to be seen on earth today meaning that the things we see at night these days could have happened millenniums of light years back.

Most of us are like these stars but we consider ourselves too tiny to shine light in this world. Only if you can discover your full potential and brilliance, your powers and light you can shine, then you have no reason to say you cannot be anything you want.

Your confidence will be shaken by temptations but that is just like our sun's magnitude during the day time, capturing all our vision making us see less of the twinkle, big twinkle stars that are distant or maybe even millions of light years away from us.

We are greater than we can imagine. We are stars in our own special ways. Discover your light and heat and radiate it in this cold world. You are already a star; you are shining both at night and during day time. You are already successful and the only thing left is to transform your success into a mega success.

Each and every star takes pride in who they are and this is why they are so beautiful up in the skies at night. They know that however bright the sun is, it will go to rest and their time to shine will soon show up. Keep shining and illuminate the darkness.

Let nothing hold you down. Cynics will come with foolish intelligence, but refute them by your actions. Never waste time giving them more time than they need. If possible, let other people handle small differences with them as you focus on your major roles.

Inspiring Quotes by Joshua Okello

1. Change just never happens until we act.
2. Your efforts to change a life might be a beacon of hope to others.
3. No money or power earned will ever fulfill you emotionally as the ability to help those less fortunate than you.
4. You can't simply buy a good reputation. It can only be earned by honoring your promises.
5. Finding strength in your failures is one way of being successful.
6. The mind grows only through use, and it atrophies through idleness.
7. Great entrepreneurs are those who keep hope alive even when nobody is supporting life.
8. To have faith means to proceed without plan B.
9. Planning is the key to success. Plan and again I say *Plan*.
10. A leader without a plan is like a magnet without poles.
11. When you don't get a miracle, be the miracle to someone else!
12. I am humbled by God's grace in my life. Give thanks in all conditions
13. Never sit around failing to try, go out there, try to fail, challenge yourself, learn new things and fail as fast as possible
14. The importance of having faith alongside our business plan is because it helps us overcome the hurdles of failures.
15. We are reluctant to adventure because of fear of failure yet we forget that some wish for opportunities to adventure even if they are going fail.
16. For sustainable development to function in developing countries, changes should not be bigger or more complex than they can handle.
17. Infinity should be your limit. Get repeated failures and repeated success.
18. Great leaders never make big and drastic changes, they keep them super simple.
19. Some things cannot be taught in entrepreneurship, they must be practiced and they are; risk prone, tenacity and persistence.
20. Nothing is as important as encouraging future leaders today.
21. Leadership is about dealing with people, treating them equally and building them. Your followers define you.
22. Organization's success heavily depends on its leadership.

23. It is my leadership imperfection that makes me strive towards building a better team.
24. In leadership, you never just wish. You have to act on your wishes.
25. In entrepreneurship, know that some offers are not worth taking.
26. Stop learning and jump on the implementation train.
27. As a leader, knowing is not enough, apply what you know.
28. Success is not attained by waiting, get going!
29. The only fight you will ever lose is the one you abandon. Never, ever give up.
30. Virtue is not given by money but can create money. Be good to all.
31. If you keep waiting for great ideas to arrive, they may never arrive. Be active in finding them and they'll come to you.
32. There is no higher honor we can ask for than being servants of God's people
33. Your efforts to change a life might be remembered forever.
34. Reputations are earned by honoring promises.
35. Finding strengths in your failures is one way of becoming successful.
36. Failure is part of the success equation.
37. Remember to put a smile on at least one person's face every day.
38. Great entrepreneurs keep hope alive even when nobody is supporting them
39. If the world does not understand you, pray that they will but better off if you can offer them something better to make them understand you.
40. What are you living for? Change lives through your actions and words.
41. To make a difference in one's life, you don't have to be brilliant, rich, beautiful or perfect. You just have to care.
42. Only if everybody was fired up to positively impact humanity for the best.
43. You are going nowhere as a leader without a plan
44. Leadership of any kind needs guts.
45. When you don't get a miracle, be the miracle to someone else!
46. Never sit around failing to try, go out there, try to fail, challenge yourself, learn new things and fail as fast as possible
47. I believe that I am the best the world has ever given.
48. How about writing a book on your failures? Cannot fill a book? Then you have not tried that much.

49. In a game of cards, never hold your cards too tight, get rid of the ones you do not need.
50. Network for personal growth and create more opportunities in your career.
51. Procrastination is the mother of failure
52. I have failed so many times, academically, as a leader, as an entrepreneur & that is why I am propelled to succeed.
53. It is a waste of time waiting for work to get easier, instead, get stronger
54. Sometimes it takes solitude moments to be successful. Put in the work.
55. We are blessed to bless.
56. Just remember that when you are sleeping, others are busy putting in the work.
57. It is until you are in a real crave for success that you succeed.
58. Success favors hard workers.
59. You do not have to be successful to be happy, happiness is in itself a success.
60. Success only comes when you turn your back away from the comfort zone.
61. You've got your inner shooting star that you need to let shine.
62. A mission started is a mission worth accomplishing.
63. Your greatness starts as soon as you kick away impossibilities
64. Do your employees respect you or fear you?
65. You are a star, so why fail to shine?
66. Are you giving in or attacking your challenges one at a time?
67. You are closer to success than you were yesterday
68. Be unrealistic in your dream, that is the only way to become great.
69. To lead does not mean you are a winner.
70. What is your purpose in life & are you fulfilling it?
71. What do you do with your one-hour to-and-fro work? Imagine in a month you lose forty hours on transit.
72. Never let your perfectionist thoughts bar you from success.
73. Sometimes we are deeply encouraged by the laughter we get from people never lose hope.
74. True winners and leaders embrace competition.
75. Your leadership represents your inner significance.
76. Success is infinite so win repeatedly.
77. Better the Angel you do not know than the devil you know.
78. Remember to bring a notebook and a pen to all your meetings.
79. We all want to be successful, but too reluctant to put in the work.
80. You snooze you lose.

81. I have come to realize that great leaders are great readers.
82. Business is easy, you are either making money or you are not.
83. We all knock but some do not knock loud enough to get the door open.
84. If you are too comfortable as a leader then you are probably doing the wrong thing.
85. Leaders are those who find peace in the most disturbing situation.
86. Leaders are those who know that at the end of the road, they can achieve what they want.
87. Communication contributes to over 80% of your success.
88. Leaders are those who are brave enough to act on their challenges with a hope of defeating them.
89. To be a hero, you must first defeat your weaknesses.
90. The best person to compare yourself with is who you were yesterday.
91. Success is mobile; you have to run faster than it to catch up with it.
92. If your history does not shock you, then you probably have not changed.
93. The majority of people reading this are going to waste their time the same way they did yesterday.
94. All leaders are thinkers and all thinkers are artists therefore craft your leadership style.
95. The discouraging voice is always louder than the encouraging voice. Ignore the loudest to prosper.
96. Stress is a waste of time in problems we are uncertain about.
97. The simple believe anything they are told; the prudent sift & weigh every word.
98. Stop defining yourself with failure, define yourself with possibility.
99. Failure means doing the right thing in a wrong way.
100. There is power in building confidence. Your success heavily relies on it.
101. There is nothing stronger than a voice telling you to get to work.
102. In everything you do, bring out your best.
103. I want to corrupt the minds of people with a message of hope, possibility & success!
104. Stay true to people, but above all, stay true to yourself. You are a hero!
105. The truth is, when you are getting into entrepreneurship, you do not know about the future but hope takes you there.
106. After pain comes pleasure, so keep plugging in for you are almost there

107. Let nothing hold you down from achieving your dreams. From people, race, gender, nationality and age. Make a breakthrough.
108. Success is achieved at greater risks, if you haven't risked, you haven't lived.
109. For success, you have to do things you do not want to do, read books you do not want to read and plan thing you do not want to plan.
110. Sometimes we do not have to speak the loudest to be heard.
111. Are you on the way pressing towards the mark?
112. You are the world's greatest! Just push yourself a little bit more.
113. To all entrepreneurs out there, remember that money is not everything. Build strong relationships
114. Do what you must do to succeed not what you feel like doing to succeed.
115. Leaders are those whose actions transform lives not deforming lives.
116. Leaders show the way, and also walk the journey.
117. Never bow down to competition, do what you do the best way you can.
118. Confidence is knowing that a challenge is greater than you but you choose to boldly tackle it.
119. For success, you have to let others take charge, but remember to be accountable.
120. Success is directly proportional to the work you put in.
121. Never waste your time starting if you know you are going to give up.
122. Where there is passion, there is less room to give up.
123. Confidence inspires confidence.
124. Leaders live to build others
125. Great leaders build genuine interest in other people's lives. Lead with passion.
126. Let leadership not take you away from your family and friends. You need them.
127. There is no other time to get to serious work like now.
128. We are all philosophers only that some philosophies take you closer to success than others.
129. Success exists because of people like you who are determined to achieve it. Never give up!
130. Success can only be achieved if you try.
131. Never let stress get in your way to success, you are more than a hero.
132. The beauty of being who you are is that you take control of creativity. Why copy others?

133. Some people you ignore could be your greatest resource. Be nice to all after all we are all human beings.
134. Leaders who sit pretty are destined to fail. Leadership is not easy.
135. Simplicity is one of the most neglected attributes of success. Keep it simple friends.
136. Utilize wisely your resources and you will see a lot more coming your way.
137. Never monetize your ideas, valuetize them instead. Add value to people's lives.
138. Never settle for less for they will make you worthless. Dream big, act big!
139. To be influential, you must be a communicator.
140. Forget the successes and failures of yesterday, implement your dreams today.
141. While implementing plan A, never think of plan B. Take plan A and succeed in it.
142. When you succeed, mentor others who come after you, your organization's future is in their hands.
143. Win people not by telling them your dreams but by showing through your actions.
144. To all leaders and entrepreneurs out there, play with anything else but NOT relationships!
145. Humanity should be defined as caring and loving one another.
146. Be proud of your mistakes, people are sick of fake perfections.
147. Life can be rough, let's treat one another with dignity/. We all should belong.
148. You are either a blessing to others or not. Choose to be a blessing.
149. Enthusiasm without passion leads to no good result. You have to have both to succeed.
150. Leaders are those who are driven by their dreams and fueled by their passion.
151. Cause Tsunami in your industry, disrupt the world, do something greater than you for success hides in gut-wrenching ideas.
152. The only way to be the greatest is to stop settling for less. You are worth more than you can imagine
153. View life as a champion and you will become one.
154. Leaders are motivated when people they motivate work towards their dreams.
155. To be something you've never been, it is a must you have to do something you've never done in your life.

156. Looking back at your history denies you the opportunity to focus on the future.
157. Courage to face our fears is what differentiates heroes from failures.
158. See yourself as a source to improve life in this world. A lot of lives need change.
159. Give your vision all your best and success will be with you wherever you go.
160. Leaders are those who make it their personal business to make a difference in areas they consider important.
161. The only way to kill fear is to do things you fear doing. Face your fears head on!
162. Leaders are those who understand that power of victory hides in taking chances.
163. A trustworthy leader is a leader worth trusting.
164. Nothing beats the discovery of your true potentials.
165. A lot of people dream of success but very few take the bold steps to act on their dreams.
166. Leaders are those who understand that the biggest freedom they have is to think of infinite success.
167. If you are making a decision, make a decision that will help you grow. Never limit yourself.
168. For success you have to take every second as a learning opportunity.
169. The day you know your purpose in life is the day you are halfway closer to success.
170. Those who inspire and motivate others to achieve greatness are either themselves great or on their way to greatness
171. Failure is always the closest friend, success stands at a distance and requires effort.
172. Motivate yourself today by sharing one of your success stories with at least one person.
173. Respect the journey you are going through for it leads you to your destination
174. If you choose to care less, life will give you less.
175. You've got the power to change the world, only if you truly believe in your efforts.
176. Why limit yourself if success has got no limits? Try big and succeed big!
177. Success comes just as you are almost reaching your breaking point.
178. Even leaders need love, encouragement, mentoring, prayers and support.

179. Progress is for those who understand that this is a new day without yesterday's mistakes.
180. There is a difference between believing in yourself and actually trying out what you truly believe in
181. Just like Microsoft, you cannot Excel without breaking your score field in your cells.
182. "I have been very busy lately" is such a lame excuse to give at any time. We are all busy.
183. Solve bigger problems with bigger solutions otherwise you are living to solve problems forever.
184. Symptoms of entrepreneurship bug bite; restlessness until you Succeed, hard work, dedication & hope
185. Transformation happens when you discover what matters the most & start working towards it
186. To become a millionaire, you must touch a million lives positively.
187. Success is easy when you bring the right people with you.
188. Your reputation is as important as your organization's brand. Guard both.
189. Wisdom shared is only valuable when implemented.
190. That moment when you say "I am! And nothing can stand in my way to success!"
191. People will endorse you as a genius when you passionately do the right things at the right time.
192. I know I have not touched many lives when I have to introduce myself to all.
193. If your thoughts and actions astound many, you are a philosopher.
194. Starting a business/movement is easy, keeping it going is the biggest challenge
195. All dreams can come true only if we could try just a little bit more than what we did yesterday.
196. Leaders are those who are broken but keep holding on for success is not achieved by quitters.
197. To become addicted to success is to become allergic to failure
198. Problems can be resolved quickly, if people put company interest above their own egos.
199. To all my young entrepreneurs, do not be a hater because haters fall!
200. Losing is not an option! You've come too far to lose. Keep up the good work.
201. Those whom we consider geniuses today did nothing but to risk trying. So try, you might be the next genius.
202. The worst thing in life is underrating your potentials.

203. The best confrontation to fears holding you down from success is to take risk.
204. Accepting responsibility is the mother of greatness. Be responsible
205. When opposing forces convince you to give up, that you cannot make it, stand tall for success is the only destination.
206. Success is a language spoken by hard workers.
207. In the beginning, every entrepreneur has to work hard, late, in solitude but persistence pays.
208. Success needs both mental and physical focus.
209. Never stop at anything. Even red lights turn green. Get going.
210. Believe that you are the best the world has ever seen and work on making it a reality
211. Leaders are those who give back as much as they have been blessed.
212. When growing, grow sustainably.
213. If something is impossible to others, never let their thoughts intoxicate your mindset.
214. There are sources and resources. You first have to source before you resource
215. Sometimes we have to abandon the "think big" philosophy and embrace "think small" to truly impact lives.
216. For success one must learn how to strike an equitable balance between the ideal and the practicable.
217. There is a reward in every struggle you persevere through. Never lose hope.
218. The successful are those who ignored their fears and clothed themselves in valor.
219. I've realized that there is always a long traffic to work, than traffic to church.
220. Solutions can only be reached through hard work.
221. Lead to transform, lead to impact, and lead to improve.
222. People will not believe you until they see the result. Start today and give them results tomorrow.
223. If you have never believed in yourself, this is the time to make yourself a believer
224. Success is like a naked switch, everybody can see it but they fear to turn it on for fear of electric shock
225. Our crave for success is determined by how much work we are putting to achieve it
226. Of all the resources, the most abused is time.
227. In this world, there are only two things involved, sleep and dream that you are successful or working hard to be successful.

228. The more you read, the more you learn.
229. If you have a better reason to wake up in the morning, you have a reason not to procrastinate.
230. If you are not ready to fail, you are not ready to learn. Leaders embrace failure.
231. If you are not living intentionally to succeed, you are living intentionally to fail.
232. Great leaders create ways for those who understand better.
233. The more you succeed, the more you should try to achieve, the more you fail, the more you should try to succeed
234. If you failed and you do not have a reason why you failed then you are going to fail again
235. We fail not because we lack ideas, but because we do not like to act.
236. Openly admitting your mistakes and accepting failures are good steps towards success.
237. If you are a leader and your pedal is not to the metal, then you need to revise your leadership.
238. Leaders are those who steer their followers' wagon wheels to prosperity.
239. I have come to realize that Einstein was brilliant and I am not. That is why I like to learn.
240. Leaders manage ideas, managers manage people
241. I want to light the heavens above like a shooting star at night.
242. Listening is a very important trait to success but we cannot all listen at the same time. One must talk.
243. For success, you have to let hard work be to you like oxygen is to your life.
244. If you are willing to die for your dream, then you can live for it.
245. Leaders change the game; they are never changed by the game.
246. What goes in your mind is what you give out.
247. To be successful, you have to boost your appetitive part of your soul towards success.
248. Visionary leaders repeatedly fail without losing hope.
249. We can underrate confidence as much as we want, but nothing great has ever been achieved without it.
250. A clock is always in motion, try and imitate that.
251. End of comfort zone marks the beginning of greatness.
252. The secret to success is to try one more time.
253. If it is business as usual, then something unusual is missing.
254. Leaders show the way to great inspiration not great expiration.

255. Let your actions enhance your image, be yourself. You are better off being you than anybody else.
256. The key to success is to treat your obligations as priorities not as options.
257. The beginning of success is to know your calling and to go for it.
258. Any dream we shutter today will come to haunt us in the future.
259. Kick out old habits if you want to see new habits work.
260. Success is not the end, it is a sign that you can achieve more.
261. You are here to change the world, are you changing it for the better or for the worst?
262. Let nothing hold you down! Success is there to be achieved.
263. Success is like a faucet, you have to turn it on. Sadly only a few people choose to do so.
264. If your ship has failed to come in, build your own. Leaders are those who take action.
265. We all have equal shares to be the greatest we ever want to be.
266. Success is always celebrated by many; failure belongs to only one person.
267. Never let your future resemble your past.
268. Were you a blessing today? And how did you bless those who needed your blessings?
269. When life pushes you to the wall, create a hole on it and move on!
270. Your personal story is the coolest you can ever tell to someone. Be yourself.
271. To move forward, you have to move backwards.
272. A lot of people try to find the way to success but they do not have a map to take them there.
273. Dreamers are slumbers. For success you have to wake up.
274. You do not have to be energetic to lead but rather energize people.
275. Finding the right coach or mentor will spin your life around.
276. To make your mark in this world, you should expect a lot of failures but never give up.
277. There is power in resilience.
278. Always go for breakthrough, not breakdown.
279. Negative mindsets are also important. They remind you of how great you are.
280. I always want to defeat who I am.
281. Leadership is the ability to transform pain into power.
282. Mohamed Ali said "He was the world's greatest," And so can you

283. To understand, we have to understand that we didn't understand
284. Dare to go past your limits this week for greater success
285. Leaders learn by teaching, think by writing.
286. Leadership is about influencing and adding value to other people's lives.
287. Leaders are people who identify and inspire others to be what they want to be.
288. Leadership today needs strategy.
289. Of all the things, never lose the big picture; it is your GPS to success.
290. Leaders inspire others to inspire
291. Failing is the only easiest thing to achieve in the entire world. It needs no effort.
292. Successful leaders build work rhythms. Do you have yours?
293. A leader is anyone who believes that they are destined to do great things.
294. Giving up is the greatest human weakness, it can only result in failure.
295. Act in faith, hope will take you miles near where success hides.
296. Stop dreaming, wake up, the implementation wagon is leaving
297. To get to the impossible, try and go slightly past the possible.
298. As a leader be ready to help others grow.
299. As a cactus stays green in a dessert, a leader should stay optimistic at all times.
300. Dwelling on the past is a waste of time. Focus on the future. That is where success hides

Index